Intelligent mobile agents E learning systems

By,
Chellatamilan T

ACKNOWLEDGMENTS

I would like to express my deepest gratitude to my supervisor, **Dr.R.M.Suresh**, Principal, Sri Muthukuamaran Institute of Technology, Chennai for his support, encouragement, guidance, and the valuable suggestions in all the related activities relevant to my research work.

I would like to thank the doctoral committee members **Dr.S.Thamarai Selvi** Dean, Madras Institute of Technology, Anna University Chennai and **Dr.L.Ganesan**, Professor and Head, Department of Computer Science and Engineering , Alagappa Chettiar College of Engineering and Technology, Karikkudi .They are always willing to help and give their best suggestions .My research would not have been possible with out their help.

I would personally like to thank my parents. They are always supporting me and encouraging me with their best wishes.

I would like to thank my wife **Mrs.K.Santhi and my children..**

Finally, I thank **Er.E.V.Kumaran**, Vice-Chairman, Arunai Engineering College for providing me the infrastructure and facility for undertaking my research experiments

T. CHELLATAMILAN

TABLE OF CONTENTS

CHAPTER NO.   **TITLE**   **PAGE NO.**

	ABSTRACT	iii
	LIST OF TABLES	xiii
	LIST OF FIGURES	xv
	LIST OF SYMBOLS AND ABBREVIATIONS	xviii
1	**INTRODUCTION TO E-LEARNING AND IR**	1
	1.1 E-LEARNING	1
	1.2 TEN PRINCIPLES OF E-LEARNING	2
	1.3 STRATEGIES FOR E-LEARNING	3
	1.4 ADVANTAGES AND DISADVANTAGES OF E-LEARNING	6
	1.4.1 Advantages of e-learning to Trainer	7
	1.4.2 Disadvantages of e-learning to Trainer	7
	1.4.3 Disadvantages of e-learning to Learner	8
	1.5 INFORMATION RETRIEVAL	9
	1.6 INFERENCE NETWORK MODEL	12
	1.7 INFORMATION RETRIEVAL SYSTEM	13
	1.8 NATURAL LANGUAGE PROCESSING	17
	1.9 MOTIVATION AND PROBLEM STATEMENT	18
	1.10 OBJECTIVES OF THE THESIS	20
	1.11 ORGANIZATION OF THE CHAPTERS	21
2	**LITERATURE SURVEY**	23
	2.1 INTRODUCTION	23

CHAPTER NO.	TITLE	PAGE NO.

2.2 E-LEARNING   23

2.2.1 Evaluating the e-Learning Standards   26

2.2.2 Aviation Industry CBT Committee (AICC)   26

2.2.3 Dublin Core Metadata Initiatives (DCMI)   27

2.2.4 ARIADNE   29

2.2.5 Advance Distributed Learning initiative   29

2.2.6 Sharable Content Object Reference

Model (SCORM)   30

2.2.7 Instructional Management System (IMS)   30

2.2.8 IEEE LTSC   30

2.2.9 Learning Object Metadata (LOM)   32

2.2.10 Learning Technology System

Architecture (LTSA)–Reference Model   34

2.2.11 Platform and Media Profiles   38

2.3 DOCUMENT CLUSTERING AND RANKING   39

2.4 INFORMATION RETRIEVAL SYSTEMS   43

2.5 LANGUAGE MODELLING   48

2.6 CONCEPT-BASED APPROACHES IN

INFORMATION RETRIEVAL   54

3 DYNAMIC NOMINAL LANGUAGE

MODEL FOR IR   60

3.1 INTRODUCTION   61

3.2 LANGUAGE MODELLING IN IR   61

3.2.1 Language Model Based on Markov Process 61

3.2.2 Language Model Based on

Bernoulli Process   61

3.2.3 Language Model Based on multinomial   64

CHAPTER NO.		TITLE	PAGE NO.

		3.2.4 Language Model Based on Poisson Process	62
		3.2.5 Smoothing	63
		3.2.6 Query Likelihood Model	63
	3.3	QUERY LIKELIHOOD RETRIEVAL METHOD	64
		3.3.1 Query Reformulation and Expansion	66
		3.3.2 Query Reformulation Algorithms	66
	3.4	NOMINAL LANGUAGE MODEL	66
	3.5	RETRIEVAL METRICS PRECISION – RECALL	67
	3.6	METHODOLOGY	68
		3.6.1 DATASETS	69
		3.6.1.1 Reuters -21578 Dataset	69
		3.6.1.2 Movilens Dataset	70
		3.6.2 Inverse Document Frequency	71
		3.6.3 Proposed tf/idf with Concept Expansion	74
		3.6.4 Dynamic Nominal Language Model	77
		3.6.4.1 Stag Affinity Ratio	78
		3.6.4.2 Score Specific Ratio	80
		3.6.4.3 Net-Affinity Rate	80
	3.7	EXPERIMENTAL SETUP AND RESULTS	82
	3.8	CONCLUSION	88
4		CLUSTER BASED FEATURE SELECTION USING HYBRID PSO	89
	4.1	INTRODUCTION	89
	4.2	CLUSTERING	91
	4.3	METHODOLOGY	92
		4.3.1 Feature Selection Methods	92
		4.3.1.1 Filter Method	92

CHAPTER NO.		TITLE	PAGE NO.

		4.3.1.2 Wrapper Method	93
		4.3.1.3 Hybrid Method	95
	4.3.2	Procedure of Feature Selection Evaluation	96
	4.3.3	Clustering for Feature Selection	97
	4.3.4	Particle Swarm Optimization	99
	4.3.5	Genetic Algorithm For Clustering	103
	4.3.6	Proposed Methodology	107
4.4		EXPERIMENTAL SETUP AND RESULTS	109
4.5		CONCLUSION	115
5		**CONCEPT BASED QUERY EXPANSION**	116
5.1		INTRODUCTION	116
5.2		QUERY EXPANSION	116
	5.2.1	Applications of AQE	119
		5.2.1.1 Question answering	119
		5.2.1.2 Multimedia information Retrieval	199
		5.2.1.3 Information filtering	120
		5.2.1.4 Cross-language information retrieval	120
		5.2.1.5 Other applications of AQE	120
	5.2.2	AQE Process	121
	5.2.3	Methods of AQE	123
5.3		DOCUMENT RANKING WITH AQE	125
5.4		PROPOSED CONCEPT BASED QUERY EXPANSION	126
5.5		EXPERIMENTAL SETUP AND RESULT	130
5.6		CONCLUSION	137

CHAPTER NO.	TITLE	PAGE NO.

6   MOBILE AGENTS BASED
**   INFORMATION RETRIEVAL**   138

6.1   INTRODUCTION   138

6.2   RELATED WORKS   139

6.3   MOBILE AGENTS   142

    6.3.1   Stationary Agents   143

    6.3.2   Mobile Agent   143

    6.3.3   Characteristics of Mobile Agents   143

6.4   MOBILE AGENT APPLICATION   145

    6.4.1   Multiple Agents executes a task in
        parallel: (Remote File Update)   145

    6.4.2   Controlling an Agent   146

    6.4.3   Agent is parallel execution   146

6.5   METHODOLOGY   146

    6.5.1   Collection Selections and Ranking   148

6.6   RECOMMENDATION SYSTEMS   149

6.7   EXPERIMENTAL SETUP AND RESULTS   152

    6.7.1   Limitations   159

6.8   CONCLUSION   160

7   CONCLUSIONS AND FUTURE WORKS   155

7.1   CONCLUSION   155

7.2   FUTURE WORKS   157

APPENDIX I   **164**

APPENDIX II   **175**

REFERENCES   182

LIST OF PUBLICATIONS   199

CURRICULUM VITAE   201

LIST OF TABLES

TABLE NO.	TITLE	PAGE NO.
3.1	Precision values for various techniques for Movielens dataset	83
3.2	Average F measure values for various techniques for Movielens dataset	85
3.3	Precision values for various techniques for Reuters 21758 dataset	86
3.4	Average F measure values for various techniques for Reuters 21758 dataset	87
4.1	Precision values for various techniques for Movielens dataset	110
4.2	Average F measure values for various techniques for Movielens dataset	111
4.3	Precision values for various techniques for Reuters 21758 dataset	112
4.4	Average F measure values for various techniques for Reuters 21758 dataset	114
5.1	Precision values for various techniques for Movielens dataset	130
5.2	Average F measure values for various techniques for Movielens dataset	131
5.3	Precision values for various techniques for Reuters 21758 dataset	133

TABLE NO.	TITLE	PAGE NO.
5.4	Average F measure values for various techniques for Reuters 21758 dataset	134
5.5	Percentage Improvement in Precision for Movielens dataset	135
5.6	Percentage Improvement in Precision for Reuters dataset	136
6.1	Precision values for various techniques for Movielens dataset	152
6.2	Average F measure values for various techniques for Movielens dataset	154
6.3	Precision values for various techniques for Reuters 21758 dataset	155
6.4	Average F measure values for various techniques for Reuters 21758 dataset	156
6.5	Precision values for various techniques for e-learning dataset	157
6.6	Average F measure values for various techniques for e-learning dataset	158
A.1.1	Literature Survey Research Table I	164
A2.1	Literature Survey Research Table I	175

LIST OF FIGURES

FIGURE NO.	TITLE	PAGE NO.
1.1	The IR System Family	10
1.2	The process of retrieving information	11
1.3	A Typical IR system	13
1.4	Retrieval Models	14
1.5	Flowchart of the Proposed Methodology	21
2.1	The LTSA abstraction-implementation layers	35
2.2	The LTSA system components	36
3.1	Retrieval Metrics	67
3.2	Flowchart of proposed methodology	68
3.3	Term frequency matrix showing frequency of terms per document	72
3.4	Relation between the df_t and idf_t for a total of million documents	73
3.5	Relation among concepts	75
3.6	Precision values for various techniques For Movielens dataset	84
3.7	Average F measure values for various Techniques for Movielens dataset	85
3.8	Precision values for various techniques for Reuters 21758 dataset	86
3.9	Average F measure values for various techniques for Reuters 21758 dataset	87
4.1	Hybrid filter and wrapper model feature Selection method	95

FIGURE NO.	TITLE	PAGE NO.
4.2	Flowchart of the proposed Hybrid Algorithm incorporating GA and PSO.	109
4.3	Precision values for various techniques for Movielens dataset	110
4.4	Average F measure values for various techniques for Movielens dataset	111
4.5	Precision values for various techniques for Reuters 21758 dataset	113
4.6	Average F measure values for various techniques for Reuters 21758 dataset	114
5.1	Main steps of automatic query expansion.	121
5.2	Precision values for various techniques for Movielens dataset	131
5.3	Average F measure values for various techniques for Movielens dataset	132
5.4	Precision values for various techniques for Reuters 21758 dataset	133
5.5	Average F measure values for various techniques for Reuters 21758 dataset	134
5.6	Percentage Improvement in Precision for Movielens dataset	136
5.7	Percentage Improvement in Precision for Reuters dataset	137
6.1	Mobile Agents in a Network	147
6.2	Precision values for various techniques for Movielens dataset	153
6.3	Average F measure values for various techniques for Movielens dataset	154

xvii

FIGURE NO.	TITLE	PAGE NO.
6.4	Precision values for various techniques for Reuters 21758 dataset	155
6.5	Average F measure values for various techniques for Reuters 21758 dataset	156
6.6	Precision values for various techniques for e-learning dataset	158
6.7	Average F measure values for various techniques for e-learning dataset	159

LIST OF ABBREVATIONS

ADL	-	Advanced Distributed Learning
AQE	-	Automatic Query Expansion
AVICC	-	Aviation Industry CBT Committee
CASE	-	Council for Advancement and Support of Educations
CBT	-	Computer Based Teaching
CLIR	-	Cross Language Information Retrieval
CPI	-	Correlation Preserving Indexing
DAS	-	Distributed Agent Systems
DCMI	-	Dublin Core Meta data Initiative
DOI	-	Document Object Identifier
ELDA	-	Event Driven Light Weight Distilled State charts based Agents
e-learning	-	Electronic Learning
FCA	-	Formal Concept Analysis
GA	-	Genetic Algorithms
IEEE LTSC	-	IEEE Learning Technology Standard Committee
IF	-	Information filtering
IMS	-	Instructional Management Systems
IR	-	Information Retrieval
IRF	-	Interactive Relevance Feedback
KPI	-	Key Performance Indicators
LCMS	-	Learning Content Management Systems
LMS	-	Learning Management Systems
LOM	-	Learning Object Metadata
LOR	-	Learning Object Repository

LTSA	-	Learning Technology Standard Committee Architecture
m-learning	-	Mobile Learning
NIST	-	National Institute for standards and Technology
NLM	-	Nominal Language Model
NTCIR	-	National Institute of Informatics Test Collection for IR Systems
PRF	-	Pseudo Relevance Feedback
PSO	-	Particle Swarm Intelligence
PSO	-	Particle Swarm Intelligence
QA	-	Question Answering Systems
RF	-	Relevance Feedback
SCORM	-	Sharable Content Object Reference Model
SVM	-	Support Vector Machine
TF-IDF	-	Term Frequency – Inverse Document Frequency
TLIR	-	Translingual Information Retrieval
TREC	-	Text Retrieval Conference

CHAPTER 1

INTRODUCTION TO e-LEARNING AND INFORMATION RETRIEVAL

1.1   e-LEARNING

Intentional use of electronic media and Information and Communication Technologies (ICT) in teaching and learning process (Naidu 2006) is referred to as e-learning, where "e" denotes "electronic". It can also be described by many other terms including online learning, virtual learning, distributed learning, network and web based learning. e-learning includes all educational activities carried out by individuals/groups working online/offline and synchronously/asynchronously through network/standalone computers and electronic devices.

Individualized self-paced e-learning - online refers to situations where individual learners access learning resources like database or course content online through Intranet/Internet. Individualized self-paced e-learning - offline is about a learner using learning resources like database/computer-assisted learning packages.

Group-based e-learning synchronously means situations where learner groups work together in real time through Intranet/Internet. Group-based e-learning asynchronously means situations where learners work over an Intranet/Internet with participants exchanges occur with a time delay.

e-learning (Marković 2010) enables higher interactivity among professors and students and study material coverage in both undergraduate/graduate students. Further, professors and assistants ensure that students' critical thinking is developed, and to provide them freedom in discussion, topics choice, exchange of ideas and information, and expansion of knowledge.

As the development of technology grows, e-learning helps students in their studies in an easy manner, anytime and anywhere. e-Learning has become a popular and acceptable way to study due to its flexibility and better innovativeness regarding introduction of new/contemporary programs as compared to traditional faculty.

Also, many faculty who opted for e-learning started implementing various software packages supporting online learning in addition to application of different studying modalities.

1.2   TEN PRINCIPLES FOR SUCCESSFUL e-LEARNING

Principle 1: Match to the Curriculum (Anderson, et al., 2005): Pedagogy should match and be aligned with appropriate curriculum via clear objectives; content relevance; student activity appropriateness and nature of the assessment.

Principle 2: Inclusion: Pedagogy should include practice seen regarding different types/range of achievement and physical disabilities which can be specifically supported by e-learning.

Principle 3: Learner Engagement: Learners should be engaged and motivated by pedagogy.

Principle 4: Innovative Approaches: The reason of learning technologies rather than non-technological approach leadings to similar end used should be evident. e-learning should suit specific purposes.

Principle 5: Effective Learning: This can be demonstrated through many ways; using various approaches in the learning platform to permit a student to choose what suits him/her.

Principle 6: Formative Assessment: Pedagogy should ensure formative assessment.

Principle 7: Summative Assessment: This must be valid and reliable, and handle various achievement levels; it should also be free from learner's adverse emotional impact.

Principle 8: Coherence, Consistency & Transparency: Student activity and assessment should match each other and pedagogy should be internally coherent/consistent in matching objectives and content.

Principle 9: Ease of Use: e-learning should ensure ease of use and transparency.

Principle 10: Cost-Effectiveness: Technology solutions should be justifiable /affordable with sustainable costs.

1.3   STRATEGIES FOR e-LEARNING

(i)   The e-learning must be participant centered.

(ii) A case must be made when value is not obvious and when point to data needs assessment. Presentation of a problem/case to participants improves clarity.

(iii) The program must ensure opportunities for success and not failure/uncertainty. To motivate/maintain involvement participants should nurture self-efficacy.

(iv) Make it real to ensure that programs should match audience in both topic/level.

(v) As e-learning relies on involvement/generosity, reveal what participation will result in.

(vi) Make it active/thought-provoking: A virtual coach reveals choices pointing out missed opportunities.

(vii) Make it human: Showcase people/emotions/successes. Reveal how people feel about what can be learnt /achieved.

(viii) Guide/track participants: Controlled experiments indicate that when novel information is dealt with, learners must be taught what and how to do.

(ix) Situate e-learning within a blend: A blended experience transcends a single experience scheduled for a specific time/place.

(x) Relationships, collaboration and teaming should be part of effort as the idea of an online community is now increasingly important.

(xi) Make it WOW! Which is when everything comes together to generate something dramatic, compelling, valued, and authentic. Something that attracts participants and involves them.

(xii) Measure and continuously improve e-learning and learning management systems (LMSs) ensure executives are comfortable with technology-based information on compliance/risk avoidance (Allison, et al., 2008).

When forming roles and responsibilities within learning systems, current and future directions should first be identified. This is done by first considering traditional learning actors roles. Two important categories of e-learning (Simic et al 2011) are experiential (significant) learning, and cognitive (meaningless) learning. Many methods contribute to effective knowledge building, but many also keep projects/problem-based learning as the cynosure. Problem solving techniques called problem-based learning can engage learners in knowledge building actively.

In addition to problem and project-based learning, similar learning methods including active learning, inquiry-based learning and service learning exist. As regards active learning, to ensure active involvement in a learning process, students should perform analysis, synthesis and evaluation, which means that listening alone is not enough. Active learning requires active part in comprehension by discussing, writing, playing simulation game roles and problem solving for learners. Inquiry-based learning recognizes that science topics are question-driven and open-ended to understand which, learners have to learn how to pose questions, perform investigations and obtain results from this basic aspect of science.

Based on software communication characteristics and resources for e-learning, three different e-learning environments are distinguished:

(i)   Self-study,

(ii)   Asynchronous, and

(iii)   Synchronous.

1.4   ADVANTAGES AND DISADVANTAGES OF e-LEARNING

e-learning applications/processes (Anand et al 2012) include computer-based, web-based and technology based learning, in addition to virtual education opportunities. Content delivery is through internet/ intranet/ extranet and audio or video tape, satellite TV, and CD-ROM including media as text, image, animation and video and audio streaming.

e-learning's main attribute is more to access information/resources. This refers to the access of information/resources any time, any place or any pace based on one's convenience. Another characteristic is access of multimedia based resources. They are various media types like text, audio, video, animation, graphics, picture in network and communication technology are supported, and which ensure information access by not only text/pictures but also through supported animations, videos, presentations and audio.

Currently e-learning is a highly emerging knowledge tool, providing a method to deliver knowledgeable contents through CD, DVD, multimedia and other tools. Its main drawback is availability of bandwidth, e-learners willingness, and skill sets to deliver material to learners.

For most regions, e-learning did not just open up "existing learning structures/content to new customers". Many regions emphasized e-learning's new methodological potential to "transform learning process", its advantages being its greater interactivity, connectivity, adaptability, and capacity to promote digital and key skills.

1.4.1 Advantages of e-learning to the Trainer or Organization

The advantages of e-learning include

(i) **Reduced overall cost** is the major factor in adopting e-learning. Reduced time away from the job may be it's a positive offshoot.

(ii) **Consistent content delivery** is possible through asynchronous, self- paced e-learning.

(iii) **Expert knowledge** is communicated and also captured through e- learning and knowledge management systems.

(iv) **Proof of completion and certification,** which are major training initiative elements, can be automated.

(v) **On-demand availability** ensures that students complete training during off-hours/from home.

(vi) **Self-pacing** for slow/quick learners increases satisfaction and lowers stress.

1.4.2 Disadvantages to the Trainer or Organization

(i) **Up-front investment** for an e-learning solution is high because of development costs. Budgets/cash flows should be negotiated.

(ii) **Technology issues** decide whether current technology infrastructure can accomplish training goals, whether it justifies additional tech expenditure and whether software/hardware compatibility is possible.

1.4.3 Disadvantages to the Learner

(i) **Technology issues** of learners are usually technophobia/unavailability of needed technologies.

(ii) **Portability** of training is e-learning's strength due to proliferation of network linking points, notebook computers, PDAs and mobile phones.

Web-based learning environments (Kybartaite et al 2009) are of 2 types: synchronous and asynchronous. A synchronous learning environment is where an instructor teaches a traditional class with the instructor and students being online simultaneously, communicating with each other. Software tools for this learning type include audio conferencing, video conferencing, and virtual whiteboards ensuring that instructors and students share knowledge.

In asynchronous learning environment, instructor interacts with students intermittently and not in real time. Asynchronous learning is support technologies like online discussion groups, email, and online courses.

e-learning environments provide the following management, development and delivery of e-learning (Kybartaite, et al., 2009) capabilities:

(i) Map Competencies to Courses: An administrator knows competencies (skills) required for specific jobs in an organization; describing learning content (courses) that teach that skill.

(ii) Schedule Classes/Register Students: An administrator schedules synchronous classes/ posts links to asynchronous class courses. Students can register for either synchronous or asynchronous classes.

(iii) Track Learning: The system tracks classes a student takes and how he scores in class assessments.

(iv) Develop Learning Content: Authors are given software tools to create asynchronous courses consisting of reusable learning objects.

(v) Deliver Learning Content: Asynchronous courses or individual learning objects stored in the server are delivered to students via a Web browser client.

Collaborative issues in which e-learning communities unfold are characterized as complex as it requires negotiation/communication to uncover. It requires high reflexivity and involves collaborative (self/peer/tutor) assessment processes. Designing and facilitation of education approaches are sensitive to specific pedagogical cultures and educational traditions. Designing teaching and learning mediated across virtual/physical spaces in higher education contexts also come within its ambit.

1.5   INFORMATION RETRIEVAL (IR)

Information Retrieval (IR) includes locating unstructured (text) material (documents) which satisfies information need from large collections (stored on computers). Information Retrieval systems are distinguished by their operational scale. It is being useful to understand 3 prominent scales. The system searches more than a billion documents in millions of computers in a web search. Personal information retrieval is at the other extreme. Recently, consumer operating systems have integrated information retrieval.

The space for enterprise, institutional and domain-specific search (Dinh and Tamine 2012), where retrieval is possible for collections like a corporation's internal documents, patents database or research articles on biochemistry is in between.

Information Retrieval is locating from a large collection, documents that fulfill a specific information need. Much Information Retrieval research concerns proposing and testing methodologies to perform this job. It can be considered that a formal relationships model between queries, documents, meaning and relevance can be used as a base for information retrieval. There can be no such model as humans cannot be left out of the equation, and yet cannot be modeled. Information retrieval techniques account for language, culture and behavior. For example, similarity estimation was circumscribed or bounded, as in cosine measure. Experiments are reliant on a standard test,but the aim is to measure users, and hence data over which prior knowledge could be asserted should be chosen so that it is not constrained by prior failures. This is important, as variables should not be present in systems: as effectiveness measurements must be controlled.

	Search by Navigation (following links as in a subject directory and the web generally)	Search by query (as in Google)	Creating answers and new information by analysis and inference-based on query
Unstructured information (text, images, sound)	**Hypermedia systems**(Many small units such as paragraph and single images tied together by links)	IR Systems (Often dealing with whole documents such as books and journal articles)	
Structured information		**Database Management Systems(DBMS)**	**Data analysis systems Expert Systems**

Figure 1.1The IR System Family

Two distinctions are of importance:

    (i) An unstructured information system deals with issues like the Reformation's economic impact.

    (ii) Finding versus creating answers. IR/database systems only locate what is already in existence.

IR has traditionally concentrated on locating entire documents which include written text; much IR research specifically focuses on text retrieval. IR is computerized retrieval of machine readable text sans human indexing.

Information retrieval systems deal with huge data amounts and should be able to process gigabytes or even terabytes of text. It should build and maintain an index for millions of documents.

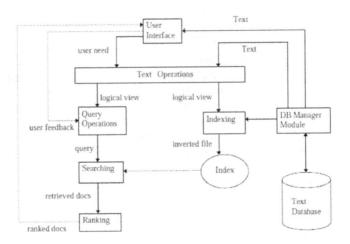

Figure 1.2 **The process of retrieving information**

1.6 INFERENCE NETWORK MODEL

Document retrieval is modeled through an inference process in an inference network, in this model. Most IR system techniques are implemented through this model (Boughanem, et al., 2009). In this model's implementation, a term is instantiated with certain strength by a document and credit from multiple terms is gathered following a query to compute a numeric score equivalent for the document. From an operational perspective, a term's instantiation strength for a document is considered the term's weight in the document, and simple document ranking in this model is similar to vector space model ranking and probabilistic models described. A term's instantiation strength for a document is not model defined and so any formulation can be utilized.

Natural Language Processing (NLP) enhances retrieval effectiveness, with limited success. Document ranking is a critical IR application, but it is not the only one as many techniques have been developed to attack varied issues including information filtering, topic detection and tracking (or TDT), speech retrieval, cross-language retrieval, question answering etc.

IR documents (Greengrass 2000) are partly structured, e.g., it has a structured header and unstructured body. The header has metadata, i.e., data about document, instead of the document's information content. For example, a book's structure consists of certain components due to it being a book, e.g., it contains title page, chapters, etc. IR retrieves documents based on unstructured components content. An IR request (called a "query") may specify a document's structured and unstructured components characteristics for retrieval.

1.7 INFORMATION RETRIEVAL SYSTEMS

IR tries to locate documents in a collection "about" a given topic or which satisfies a specific information need. Topic or information need is expressed through a user generated query. According to users, documents which satisfy a query are "relevant" and those not about a topic is "non-relevant". A query may be used by an IR engine to classify a documents collection (or in an incoming stream), returning a documents subset which meets some classification criterion for the user. The higher the proportion of user returned documents that are relevant, the better the classification criterion (Kelly 2009). Figure 1.3 reveals a typical IR system.

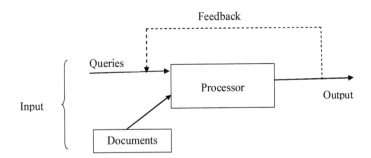

Figure 1.3 A Typical IR system

Relevance judgments effectiveness is quantified by two measures: recall (relevant documents number identified by a subject for a query divided by total relevant documents, within examined ones, for the query), and judgments precision.

Most automatic information retrieval systems are experimental in nature. Experimental IR is usually tried out in 'laboratory' situations whereas those which are operational are commercial, charging for their services. Both systems are evaluated differently. 'Real world' IR systems are evaluated regarding 'user satisfaction' and the price a user pays for services. Experimental IR systems evaluation is by comparing retrieval experiments with specially constructed standards.

Retrieval Model

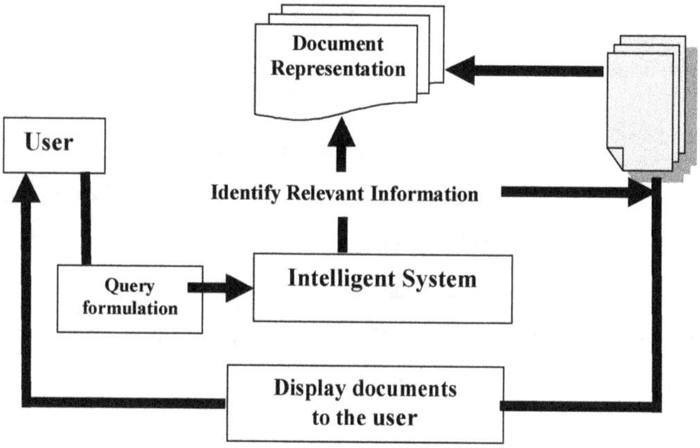

Figure 1.4 Retrieval models

Information storage and retrieval are simple in principle, if there is a document cluster and a person (user) formulates a question (request or query) for which a document set is the answer, satisfying his question's information need.

When high speed computers were available for non-numerical work, many felt a computer could 'read' an entire document collection to extract relevant documents. It soon was apparent that use of a document's natural language text not only resulted in input and storage problems, it also left unsolved document content characterizing problems. Future hardware developments may ensure feasible natural language input and storage. Automatic characterization where software tries to duplicate human 'reading' process is a very sticky issue. Specifically, 'reading' involves extracting information - both syntactic and semantic - from text to decide whether a document is relevant to a particular request. The difficulty is in extracting information and using it to decide relevance. Modern linguistics slow progress on the semantic front and machine translation's failure reveal that such issues are yet unsolved.

Literature presents three IR models (Vinciarelli 2005): the first being called Boolean, the second is Vector Space Model (VSM) and the third is called probabilistic. Boolean model is based on binary algebra: queries being expressed as logical conditions. Probabilistic approaches estimate a document's probability being relevant to a specific query. This needs many training queries which are hard to get.

Documents are represented as vectors in Vector Space Model (VSM) and their relevance to user queries is measured by appropriate matching functions (Tsatsaronis and Panagiotopoulou 2009). There are two major components in the IR process: the first is term extraction by a document matrix performed for a given database, once. The second is document identification as relevant to a query and performed every time a query is submitted.

The term by document matrix 'A' is obtained through many steps: preprocessing, normalization and indexing. Preprocessing removes elements not useful in retrieval.

Normalization removes variability not useful to retrieval and is performed through two steps: stopping and stemming. During stopping, all words which have poor index terms (stopwords) are removed. Stemming is replacing different inflected forms of certain words with their stems.

In Information retrieval systems (Sanderson and Croft 2012) started electro-mechanical searching devices, adoption of computers to locate user query relevant items. Both electro-mechanical and computer-based IR systems search style is Boolean retrieval. A query is a logical term (a synonym to word in IR literature), which result in a documents set that match the query exactly. An alternative approach is where each collection of document is given, a score to indicate its relevance to a query. This ranked retrieval search approach was taken up by IR researchers, who over decades refined and revised documents sorting regarding a query. This approach effectiveness over Boolean search was proved over the years.

Information retrieval systems (Sanderson and Zobel 2005) effectiveness is measured by comparing performance on a common queries set and documents. Many tests evaluated such comparison's reliability.

Test collections are used for retrieval systems comparison and evaluation. These collections comprising of documents, queries (or topics), and relevance judgments are key Information Retrieval (IR) research for years; collections are based on research or practice in collection formation and retrieval effectiveness measurement. Effectiveness computation is madeby measuring systems relevant documents location ability. The measured score indicates a system's performance relative to another; it is being assumed that similar relative performance is observed on other test collections operational settings.

1.8   NATURAL LANGUAGE PROCESSING (NLP)

Natural Language Processing (NLP) (Krallinger et al 2005) is where computers are used to process language including techniques to provide basic methodology for automatic relevant information extraction from unstructured data, like scientific publications. Information retrieval and NLP systems are likely to become important for both information extraction and assisting in research's various aspects like new facts discovery, findings interpretation, and experiments design. Though useful for many jobs, such tools consume time when used for efficient searches and article selection, such functions being repeated regularly to update knowledge.

Identification of entities in free text in NLP is called Named-Entity Recognition (NER). To identify biological entities like genes, proteins and drugs automatically within free text, over fifty information-extraction/text-mining tools were recently implemented with two community-wide evaluations being carried out.

When a document collection is obtained, clues are given for documents to be retrieved from a collection. Then documents matching clues are answers to a query. In invoking a search engine, a few words are presented which are matched to stored documents, the best matches being the responses. The process is generalized to a document matcher, where instead of few words a complete document becomes the clue. Input document is matched with all stored documents, with best matching documents being retrieved.

A basic information retrieval concept is measuring similarity between two documents. For this, a small word set input into a search engine is considered, a document to be matched to others. Measuring similarity is related to predictive methods for learning/classifying methods. Measuring similarity is a common theme, and the method's variations are basic to information retrieval.

1.9   MOTIVATION AND PROBLEM STATEMENT

The advent of internet technology to share educational contents and experiences ensured that institutions globally, offered a federated search to courses, lesson plans, contents, assignments, seminars and experiments, all of which are stored in repositories of learning content management systems controlled by a learning management system. The problem faced by a learner's community is in accessing, sharing and delivering quality relevant to content for online teaching learning systems. Today peer to peer networks are used for daily sharing of videos, audios, images, music or other distributed learning digital processes. Hence, sophisticated search and information retrieval solutions are necessary. Many existing web based course structures developed in e-learning system are considered as course ontology and can be mapped into a model. This ontology based solution increases information retrieval accuracy through high precision and recall.

Language Model defines documents probability distribution using them to predict likelihood of query terms observation. Language model has been defined for all documents and it is used to inquire about chances of query generation. Nominal Language Model (NLM) based language modelling goes with part of speech of a given query's literal language, constituting factors with noun and adjectives. Informational query attempts to capture a document with data, relevant to analysis area. NLM based Information Retrieval process is an efficient method to extract relevant documents. Language modelling is processed with natural language processing methods.

A term/phrase can have many meanings, while a domain specific concept is unambiguous. It is useful to use the domain specific concepts in documents than terms to retrieve documents from a specific domain. In this proposal, NLM is assembled with rate specifications and ratio calculations through use of probabilistic terms involving comparing query terms occurrence with data store using conditional probability theorem.

Feature selection in classification is being viewed as a most fundamental issue in machine learning. Data clustering is a popular data labeling technique where unlabeled data is issued, and similar samples put in one pile called a cluster with dissimilar samples being in other clusters. Data clustering, an NP-complete problem of locating groups in heterogeneous data by minimizing some dissimilarity measure is a basic tool in data mining, machine learning and pattern classification solutions.

Query expansion methods were long studied - with debatable success on many occasions. This study presents a probabilistic query expansion model based on similarity thesaurus constructed automatically. The latter reflects domain knowledge about specific collections from which it is constructed. Two important issues with query expansion are addressed here: selection and weighting of additional search terms. Compared to earlier methods, queries are expanded by addition of terms similar to query concept, instead of selecting terms similar to query terms.

Mobile Agents are independent smart programs moving through networks, seeking and interacting with available/compatible services on user's behalf. Another attractive paradigm property is that it allows an application to be really distributed, as tasks in an application, embodied in a mobile agent, are worked out on participating systems in a decentralized process.

This study addresses pre-processing and various source documents retrieval to achieve improved Information Retrieval systems and investigates tools/techniques used for autonomous classification or documents clustering; new methods are proposed based on concept expansion.

1.10   OBJECTIVES OF THE THESIS

Locating learning material groups relevant to learning goal (query), results in learning process efficiency. The scope of this thesis is in increasing content retrieval efficiency and accuracy through a query refining and reformulation method through pre-processing operations like stemming, stop word removal, dimensionality reduction and relevance feedback mechanism. Reuter's dataset and Movielens dataset are used in this research. The following summarizes the objective of the thesis:

(i)   Propose a concept expansion for creating corpus

(ii)   Propose a language modeling based on Nominal Language Model

(iii)   Propose a cluster based Feature selection method based on Particle Swarm Optimization and Genetic Algorithm

(iv)   Optimization of document clustering using proposed Mobile Agent Figure 1.5 shows the flow of the proposed methodology.

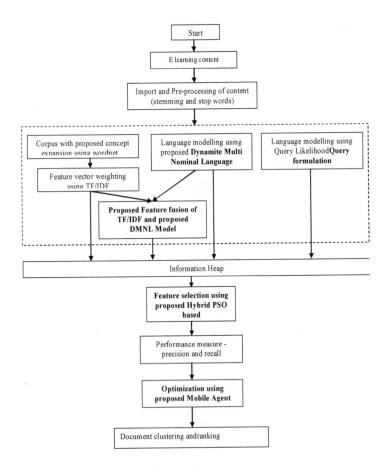

Figure 1.5 Flowchart of the Proposed Methodology

1.11 ORGANIZATION OF THE CHAPTERS

The second chapter deals with literature survey of work related to e-learning, document clustering and Ranking, IR Systems, concept based approaches in IR and language models.

The third chapter discusses in detail about various language modeling. A concept expansion for creating corpus is proposed. The evaluation on the proposed method using Reuter's dataset and MovieLens data is discussed.

The fourth chapter details with the proposed language modeling based on nominal language model.

The fifth chapter proposes a cluster based feature selection method based on Particle Swarm Optimization (PSO) and Genetic Algorithm (GA).

The sixth chapter discusses the process of optimization of document clustering using proposed mobile agent. The experimental results are explained in a detailed manner.

The seventh chapter concludes the research work.

CHAPTER 2

LITERATURE SURVEY

2.1   INTRODUCTION

This chapter deals with the review of various aspects of e-learning and Information retrieval. The papers reviewed are sectioned as follows and tabular version has been enclosed in the Annexure I and II:

(i)   e-learning

(ii)   Document clustering and ranking

(iii) Information retrieval systems

(iv) Concept-based approaches in information retrieval

(v)   Language models

2.2   e-LEARNING

Strijbos et al (2011) discussed addressing collaborative learning assessment with a perspective on what is to be assessed, highlighting current approaches and limitations. Within Computer-Supported (CS) Collaborative Learning (CL) research community; there was major dialogue on theories /perspectives on collaborative learning, scripting the collaborative process approaches, with research methodology being the most recent. Assessment of collaborative learning received less attention in contrast. As collaborative learning assessment is demanding for teachers and students adequate computer-supported and intelligent tools to monitor and assess are needed. A roadmap is presented as regards the role and application of intelligent tools for assessment of CL.

Brut et al (2011) extended IEEE LOM standard with ontology-based semantic annotations solution for use of learning objects sans Learning Management Systems. The data model which corresponds to this approach is presented first. Also, presented is a proposed indexing technique for this model's development to acquire a better learning resources annotation. Two alternative methods for structure-based indexing of textual resources are extended and combined: the latent semantic indexing mathematical approach and linguistic-oriented WordNet-based text processing. Hence, the reason behind good results due to the first method becomes transparent, because of linguistic controlled choices suggested by the second method. In the context of adopting semantic web technologies for e-learning, the results are important, and also as progress in ontology-based textual resources indexing.

An agent-based m-learning system was presented by Glavinic et al (2008). This study provides a roadmap for m-learning systems design based on agent technology. M-learning, as a "portable and personal" e-learning fashion, enhances the efficiency/effectiveness of learning in hand held terminals. Mobile intelligent tutoring systems are specific m-learning systems basing their work on a human teacher simulation in a learning/ teaching process. Systems should provide intelligent support to learners and adapt to various networks/mobile devices. Consequently this implies use of agent-based solutions as an architectural basis. The issue is lack of agent-based software development methods and common scenarios/templates to build multi-agent systems.

SWAM, a platform to build and deploy Prolog-based intelligent mobile agents on Semantic Web was presented by Crasso et al (2011). A big repository of static data, the Web has gradually become a worldwide network of information and services called Semantic Web which enables programs to interact autonomously with Web-accessible information/services. Thus, mobile agent technology helps efficiently exploit the new Web in an automated way, as Semantic Web resources are described in a computer-literate way. This article reports examples and experimental results to illustrate and assess SWAM's benefits.

Cuéllar et al (2011) developed a procedure to integrate different e-learning systems, and give semantics to Learning Management Systems (LMS) database entities or relations through ontology. Internet LMSs are tools that help in daily teaching/learning activities. Most users or the software is focused on content dissemination and group works, but internet LMS possibilities could go further. Recent approaches use semantic web to improve e-learning capabilities and user experiences through artificial intelligence and knowledge management techniques. The suggested integration eases learning resources and knowledge dissemination from LMS databases. Also, database schemes' semantic interpretations ensure location of precise information expeditiously.

A performance-oriented e-learning approach was presented by Jia et al (2011). Despite increasing workplace e-learning practices, most e-learning applications do not meet learners' needs or serve organization success quest. Major gaps between organizational interests and individual needs exist in e-learning, making such applications less goal-effective. To overcome this, Key Performance Indicators (KPIs) clarify organizational training needs in addition to helping learners establish rational learning objectives. Ontology is also used to construct formal and machine-understandable performance-oriented learning environment conceptualization.

With this approach, a KPI-oriented learning ontology and prototype system were developed /evaluated to demonstrate the approach's effectiveness.

2.2.1   Evaluation of e-learners Standards

Like all technology e-learning has evolved standards from 1994 to develop a metadata driven framework to access web resources due to discovery of electronic resources in 1997.

The National Institute for Standards and Technology (NIST) and the IEEE p.1484 study group (IEEE-LTSC-IEEE learning technology stands technology) collaborated with ARIDIVE a European project having active metadata definitions.

In 1998,Instructional Management System(IMS) and ARIADIVE submitted joint proposal/specifications to the IEEE Learning Object Metadata (LOM) base document.

2.2.2   Aviation Industry CBT Committee (AICC)

AICC is an information training professional forum to develop guidelines in the aviation industry for the development, delivery and evolution of CBT and related training technology.

AICC objectives are as follows

(i)   Developing guidelines for interoperability

(ii)   Providing open forum to describe CBT and training technology.

(iii)   Promoting economic/effective computer based training.

(iv)   Focusing on online learning reuse/interoperability.

(v) Coordinating effort with learning technology standards like Learning Technology Systems Architecture (LTSA) of IEEE and Advance Distributed Learning (ADL).

2.2.3 Dublin Core Metadata Initiatives (DCMI)

DCMI is an organization promoting adoption of interoperable metadata standards and developing specialized metadata vocabulary to describe resources enabling more intelligent information discovery systems. The fifteen elements of Dublin core semantics were established by an international, cross disciplinary group of professionals through consensus, from librarianships, computer science, text encoding, museum community and related fields.

The fifteen elements are as follows

(i) Title: A Title is a name by which resources are formally known.

(ii) Creator: An entity responsible to make resource content. For example, authors in written documents, artists, photographers, or illustrators in visual resources.

(iii) Subject and Keywords: The content topic of resource. A Subject is expressed as keywords, key phrases or classification codes describing a resource topic.

(iv) Description: An account of resource content. Description includes but not limited to, abstract, contents tables, reference to graphical content representation or content's free-text account.

(v)   Publisher: An entity responsible to make resource available.

(vi) Contributor: An entity to make contributions to resource content.

(vii) Date: Date will be associated with resource creation/ availability. Recommended best practice to encode date value is defined in ISO 8601 profile and follows YYYY-MM-DD format.

(viii) Type: Nature/genre of resource content. Type includes content terms describing general categories/ functions/ genres/ aggregation levels.

(ix) Format: This includes media-type/resource dimensions. Format may determine software/hardware or other equipment to display/operate resource. Dimension examples include size and duration.

(x)   Identifier: A reference to resource in a given context. Recommended best practice is identifying resource through a string/number in a formal identification system. Examples include Uniform Resource Identifier (URI) including Uniform Resource Locator (URL), Digital Object Identifier (DOI) and International Standard Book Number (ISBN).

(xi) Source: A reference to resource from which present resource is derived.

(xii) Language: Language of the intellectual resource content. Recommended best practice is using RFC 3066 in conjunction with ISO 639 to define two- and three-letter primary language tags with optional subtags. Examples include "en" or "eng" for English, "akk" for Akkadian, and "en-GB" for English used in the UK.

(xiii) Relation: A related resource reference.

(xiv) Coverage: Extent/scope of resource content. Coverage includes spatial location (place name/geographic coordinates), temporal period (period label, date/date range) or jurisdiction (named administrative entity).

(xv) Rights: Rights Information held in and over resource. A Rights element contains a resource's rights management statement or refers to a service giving such information. It also encompasses Intellectual Property Rights (IPR), Copyright, and various Property Rights

2.2.4 ARIADNE:

ARIADNE is a European digital library project for academic and corporate context providing access to resources and focused on tools and methodologies development to produce, manage and reuse computer based pedagogical elements based on syllabi and curricular. Ariadne and IMS jointly developed a metadata specification for submission to IEEE.

2.2.5 Advance Distributed Learning initiative (ADL)

This is US department of defense and white house office of science and technology program to develop guidelines for large scale development /implementation of efficient/effective distributed learning.

2.2.6 Sharable Content Object Reference Model (SCORM)

The US Federal government ADL initiative and recently relearned SCORM are recent examples of learning standards application and integration. This provides a foundation for learning techniques to build Operate in a future learning environment. Military, Air, Navy, Army or Marine can exchange, manage, track and review all learning content/date whatever be its source/application.

2.2.7 Instructional Management System (IMS) Global Learning Consortium

In 1997, the IMS project focused on initiatives relating to standards for learning servers, learning content and enterprise integration of such capabilities.

IMS Consortium is at an advanced stage of developing learning resources metadata specification for creation of a uniform way to describe learning resources to ensure easy focus.

To share learner's data, courses perform across platforms, operating system and user interfaces. Content Packaging Specification ensures easier creation of reusable, sharable content objects used across many learning management systems. Question and test specification address the need to share test items, and assessment tools across varied systems. IMS learner profile specification organizes learner information to ensure that learning system is responsive to learner's specific needs.

2.2.8 IEEE Learning Technology Station Committee (LTSC)

The IEEE Computer Society Standards Activity Board chartered LTSC develops accredited technical standards, recommended practices/guides for learning technology. LTSC formally/informally coordinates with other organizations which produce specifications/standards for similar purposes. Up to twenty working groups discussed various e-learning aspects at various times.

IEEE LTSC has over a dozen working groups and study group.

(i)   IEEE 1484.1 Architect and ref model

(ii)   IEEE 1484.3Glossary

(iii)   IEEE 1484.2 Learner model

(iv)   IEEE 1484.13 Student identifier

(v)   IEEE 1484.19 Quality system for lifelong learning

(vi)   IEEE 1484.10 CBT Data Exchange

(vii)   IEEE 1484.6 Course Sequencing

(viii) IEEE 1484.17 Content Packages

(ix)   IEEE 1484.12 Learn Object metadata

(x)   IEEE 1484.9 Localization

(xi)   IEEE 1484.14 Semantics and Exchange bindings

(xii)   IEEE 1484.15 Date Interchange Protocols

(xiii) IEEE 1484.11 Computer managed lasting.

(xiv)   IEEE 1484.18 Tool/Agent Communications

2.2.9   Learning Object Metadata (LOM)

LOM is an approved IEEE-SA standard passed on to ISO/IEC JTC1/SC36 to convert to international standards. LOM is based on ARIADNE, IMS and DCMI defining a structure for different granularities learning objects interoperable descriptions. A learning object is an entity digital/non-digital that is used to learn, educate or train. LOM descriptions are grouped as general, life cycle, meta-metadata, educational, technical, educational rights, relation, annotation, and classification. It doesn't define how learning technology systems represent/use metadata instance to learn an object; as partly defined in IMS and ADL/SCORM.

This standard's purpose is facilitating learning objects search, evaluation, acquisition, use, sharing and exchange by learners/ instructors /automated software processes like course authoring/structuring tools.

LOM defines nine categories to group various data elements (Hodgins and Wason 1998):

(i)   General category groups: general information describing learning object as whole, like title, language, description, keyword, coverage, structure (underlying learning object's organizational structure; e.g. atomic, linear or hierarchical) and aggregation level (granularity level – from raw media to a course set)

(ii)   Lifecycle category groups: features related to learning object's history and current state and those affected by learning object during evolution. Elements include version, status, and state of object contributors.

(iii) The Meta-Metadata category groups: metadata instance information (rather than learning object described by metadata instance). E.g. a unique record identifier, metadata contributors, metadata schema (e.g. LOMv1.0) and language

(iv) The Technical category groups: Learning object's technical requirements/characteristics. Elements are format (mime type), size, location (URL or URI), technical requirements, installation remarks, other platform requirements and duration.

(v) The Educational category groups: Learning object's key educational and pedagogic characteristics. This includes interactivity type (active learning, like an exercise/simulation vs. expositive=passive learning, like reading), learning resource type (exercise, simulation, questionnaire, diagram, figure, graph, index, narrative text), interactivity level (very low – very high), semantic density (conciseness degree), intended end user role (teacher, author, learner, manager), context (school, higher education, training), typical age range, typical learning time, description and language.

(vi) The Rights category groups: Learning object's intellectual property rights and usage conditions. It includes a cost field (yes/no), copyright (yes/no), and description.

(vii) The Relation category groups: Learning object's features defining a relationship with other related learning objects like kind (nature of relationship, e.g. is/has part of, is/has version of, is/has format of, is referenced by, is based on, is basis for, requires, is required by), resource (target learning object resource) and description.

(viii) Annotation category gives comments on learning object's educational use providing information on when and by whom comments were created. It has an entity (people, organisation who created annotation), date and description.

(ix) Classification category describes learning object with regard to specific classification system. Elements are purpose (skill level, competency, security level, educational level, discipline, idea, prerequisite, educational objective, accessibility and restrictions), a specific classification system's taxonomic path, description and keywords.

This standard facilitates search, evaluation, acquisition, use, sharing and exchange of learning objects by learners/instructors or automated software processes like course authoring and structuring.

2.2.10 Learning Technology System Architecture (LTSA) – Reference Model

This specifies a high architecture level for technology enhanced learning, education and training systems to

(i) Provide a framework to understand existing/future systems

(ii) Promote interoperability and portability through identifying abstract, high level system interface.

(iii) Incorporate a technical horizon of 5-10 years minimum while being adapting new technologies/learning technology system.

Standardisation document clarifies five refinement architecture layers, but layer three alone is normative, the remaining four layers being meant for information and completeness.

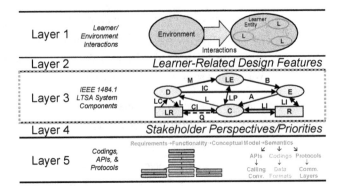

Figure 2.1 The LTSA abstraction-implementation layers

The system's five layers as seen in Figure 2.1 separate the "big picture" from "details" and help understand/analyze the system step by step. Each layer is investigated independently as they do not influence each other. They are called:

(i) Learner and Environment Interactions: Concerns learner's acquisition, transfer, exchange, formulation, discovery, etc., of knowledge and/or information through interaction with environment from information technology perspective and not a description of learning theory. It shows the learner has new/different knowledge after a learning experience.

(ii) Learner-Related Design Features: is about the effect learners have on learning technology systems, and how it is affected by learners needs specifically, the nature of human learning.

(iii) System Components (normative): Describes component-based architecture, as identified in human-centred and pervasive features. The LTSA identifies

a) four processes: learner entity, evaluation, coach, and delivery process;

b) two stores: learner records and learning resources;

c) thirteen information flows among components: behavioural observations, assessment information, learner information (thrice), query, catalogue info, locator (twice), learning content, multimedia, interaction context, and learning preferences.

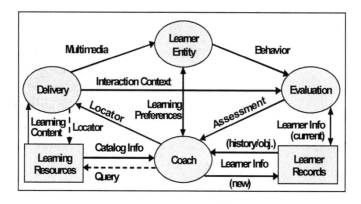

Figure 2.2 The LTSA system components

The operation has the form (Figure 2.2):

a) learning styles, strategies, methods are negotiated among learner and stakeholders and communicated as learning preferences;

b) learner is observed and evaluated regarding multimedia interactions;

c) evaluation produces assessments and/or learner information;

d) learner information is stored in learner history database;

e) coach reviews learner's assessment/information like preferences, past performance history, and, possibly, future learning objectives;

f) coach searches learning resources, through query/catalogue info, for learning content;

g) coach extracts locators from catalogue info passing locators to delivery processes, e.g., a lesson plan; and

h) Delivery process extracts learning content from learning re-sources and based on locators transforms learning content to learner through an interactive multimedia presentation.

(iv) Implementation Perspectives and Priorities: Describes learning technology systems from various perspectives through reference to system components layer subsets. Different use of e-learning systems case models are analyzed and inter-process and communication models sketched.

(v) Operational Components and Interoperability — coding's, APIs, protocols: Describes generic "plug-n-play" (interoperable) components/interfaces of information technology-based learning technology architecture, as seen in stakeholder perspectives.

Actual coding specification and API protocols standards are outside LTSA scope.

2.2.11 Platform and Media Profiles

This work group aims to identify other standards/ formats relevant to e-learning and browser platforms/media types. Standard does not describe technical details, only limitations/enhancements to referring standards. This standard specifically deals with the following issues:

(i) 1484.18.1.*: Bundles of profiles: e.g. a browser with specific capabilities set (JavaScript, Java, HTML, CSS and media type support) and plug ins

(ii) 1484.18.2.*: Markup Languages: various HTML, XML and style sheet versions.

(iii) 1484.18.3.*: Audio Formats: like wav, real audio and mp3.

(iv) 1484.18.4.*: Video and Graphics Formats: e.g. avi, quicktime, mpeg, jpeg, gif, bmp, png, flash, shockwave, cgm.

(v) 1484.18.5.*: Page Description Languages: e.g. PDF and Postscript.

(vi) 1484.18.6.*: Java: various JDK and JVM versions.

(vii) 1484.18.7.*: JavaScript: various JavaScript and ECMA script versions.

(viii) 1484.18.8.*: Word Processing Formats: e.g. RTF, Microsoft Word, WordPerfect etc.

(ix) 1484.18.9.*: Presentation Graphics: e.g. Microsoft PowerPoint.

(x) 1484.18.10.*: Spread sheet Formats: e.g. Microsoft Excel.

(xi) 1484.18.11.*: Document Services currently refers to DOM level 1.

2.3   DOCUMENT CLUSTERING AND RANKING

Sanz-Rodriguez et al (2010) tried improving recommending learning objects, this document highlighting insufficiencies of current approaches, identifying quality indicators to provide information based on which materials can be recommended to users. Next, a synthesized quality indicator to facilitate learning objects ranking, according to overall quality, is suggested. Thus, clear evaluations by users/experts are used with usage data thereby completing recommendation based information. The relationships that exist between different quality indicators in a set of learning objects from the Merlot repository were analyzed to ensure an overall quality indicator to be calculated automatically, guaranteeing rating of all resources.

Ochoa et al (2008) improved learning object search's current status. First, the situation is analyzed to propose a theoretical solution, based on relevance ranking. This study develops relevance concept in a learning object search context to implement the solution. Based on the concept, a set of metrics to estimate topical, personal and situational relevance dimensions is proposed. Metrics are calculated from usage and contextual information not needing any user information. An exploratory metrics evaluation reveals that even simple ones provide statistically significant ranking order improvement, over a most common algorithmic relevance metric. Also, combining metrics through learning algorithms sorts result list better by 50 per cent than baseline ranking.

Hristidis et al (2011) presented algorithms to return query based top results, ranked according to an IR-style ranking function, when operating on a Boolean query source interface with no ranking capabilities (or a ranking capability that did not interest end user).Many online/local data sources provide good querying mechanisms with reduced ranking facilities. For instance, PubMed permits users to submit expressive Boolean keyword queries, but ranks query results only according to date,but users prefer relevance ranking, measured by an information retrieval (IR) ranking function. A naive approach would be to submitting a disjunctive query with query keywords and to retrieve all returned matching documents, and then re-rank them. This would be expensive due to large number of disjunctive query returned results. The proposed algorithms enable conjunctive queries which return only candidate documents for relevance metric based high ranking. This process can also be applied to settings where ranking is monotonic on a factors set (query keywords in IR) and source query interface is their Boolean expression. A comprehensive evaluation on PubMed database and a Text REtrieval Conference (TREC) data set prove achievement of high order magnitude improvement when compared to existing baseline approaches.

Yen et al (2010) followed SCORM and Content Object Repository Discovery and Registration Architecture (CORDRA) specifications in developing a registry system, MINE Registry. Based on internet and search engine popularity, users request information through web based services. Though general-searching as provided by Google is powerful, metadata is needed as a searching mechanism for specific purposes. SCORM ensures efficient metadata definition for learning objects to be searched and shared in e-learning. To enable a federated repository search, CORDRA ensures a common architecture to discover/share Learning Objects. MINE Registry stores and shares 20,738 Learning Objects generated over the last five years. The concept of "Reusability Tree" to represent relevant Learning Objects relationships was proposed and enhanced CORDRA as a contribution. Relevant information was collected, when users utilized Learning Objects like citations and time period persisted. Feedbacks from users are critical elements to evaluate significance degree of Learning Objects. A mechanism to weight/rank Learning Objects in MINE Registry was proposed through such factors, in addition to external learning objects repositories. A tool called "Search Guider" is provided to assist users find relevant information in individual requirements based Learning Objects.

A new spectral clustering method called Correlation Preserving Indexing (CPI) was presented by Zhang et al (2012). This is performed in correlation similarity measure space where documents are projected into a low-dimensional semantic space within which correlations between documents in local patches are maximized while correlations between documents outside the patches are reduced simultaneously. As document space's intrinsic geometrical structure is embedded in similarities between documents, correlation as a similarity measure suits detection of intrinsic geometrical structure of document space more than Euclidean distance. Hence, the proposed CPI method effectively discovers intrinsic structures fixed in high-dimensional document space. The new method's effectiveness is demonstrated by experiments conducted on various data sets and comparing them with current document clustering methods.

Duh et al (2011) examined whether easy to obtain additional unlabelled data can improve supervised algorithms. Ranking functions are important in information retrieval systems. Recently there was much research in "learning to rank," which aims to use labelled training data and machine learning algorithms to ensure construction of reliable ranking functions. Machine learning methods like neural networks, support vector machines, and least squares were successfully applied to ranking problems, and some were already deployed in commercial search engines. Despite this, most algorithms today construct ranking functions in a supervised learning setting, assuming that relevance labels are ensured by human annotators before training a ranking function. Such methods perform poorly when human relevance judgments are unavailable for a query range. The transductive setting was specifically investigated, where unlabelled data is equal to test data. A simple, flexible transductive meta-algorithm was proposed, the idea being to adapt training procedure to test lists after observing documents that need ranking. Two instantiations of this general framework were investigated: Feature Generation approach discovers more salient features from unlabelled test data and trains a ranker on a test-dependent feature-set. The important weighting approach relies on ideas in domain adaptation literature, and works by training data re-weighting to match statistics of each test list. Both proposed approaches proved that it performs better than supervised algorithms on TREC and OHSUMED tasks from a LEarning TO Rank (LETOR) dataset.

Cai and Li (2013) proposed an approach which directly generates clusters that were integrated with ranking. The idea was that ranking distribution of sentences in each cluster should be quite different from each other, which may serve as features of clusters and new clustering measures of sentences was calculated accordingly. Also better clustering results achieves better ranking results too. As a result, performance of ranking and clustering is improved.

Navaneethakumar(2013) proposed a conceptual rule mining on text clusters to evaluate the more related and influential sentences contributing the document topic. Author has plan to extend conceptual text clustering to web documents, by assigning the sentence weights based on conditional probability. With sentence rank conceptual rules, the text cluster documents were defined. The conceptual rule depicts the finer tuned document topic and sentence meaning utilized for evaluating the global document contribution.

2.4   INFORMATION RETRIEVAL SYSTEMS

A framework to build an adaptive Learning Management System (LMS) was suggested by Yaghmaie et al (2011) based on multi-agent systems and using both Sharable Content Object Reference Model (SCORM) 2004 and semantic Web ontology to ensure learning content storage, sequencing and adaptation. This system was implemented on an open-source LMS and its functionalities demonstrated through simulation of a scenario mimicking real life conditions. The result proves the system's effectiveness and appears very promising.

Larkey et al (2005) proposed two probabilistic approaches. Cross-lingual retrieval is used today and is based on probabilistic relevance models, as exemplified by INQUERY, and on those based on language modeling. INQUERY, a query net model, ensures easy incorporation of query operators, including a synonym operator, and proved to be very useful in Cross-Language Information Retrieval (CLIR); an approach termed structured query translation. In sharp contrast, language models include translation probabilities in a unified framework. With Arabic and Spanish data sets, two approaches were compared with two kinds of bilingual dictionaries—one from a conventional dictionary, and another from a parallel corpus. Structured query processing provided slightly better results when queries were not expanded, but when queries were expanded, language modeling ensures better results, but again only when using a probabilistic parallel corpus dictionary. Two additional issues in the structured query processing comparison with language modeling were pursued. The first was regarding query expansion and the second, the role of translation probabilities. Conventional expansion techniques (pseudo-relevance feedback) was compared with relevance modeling, a new IR approach that fit into formal language modeling framework. Relevance modeling and pseudo-relevance feedback achieved comparable retrieval levels with good translation probabilities conferring a small but significant advantage.

A web-based learning support system that harnesses two approaches - learning path constructing approach and learning object recommending approach was developed by Hsieh et al (2010). Recently, browsers are popular tools for internet information searching. Though users can locate and download specific learning materials to gain fragmented knowledge, most materials are imperfect without specific content order. This results in self-directed learners spending more time surveying and choosing right learning materials from the Internet. The system discovers candidate courses using data mining based on Apriori algorithm founded on collected documents and a learning subject from learners. Next, the Formal Concept Analysis (FCA) based leaning path constructing approach, builds a Concept Lattice with keywords got from selected documents. Then a relationship hierarchy of all the concepts represented by keywords is formed. It then uses FCA to compute more mutual relationships among documents to ensure a correct learning path. The support system uses both preference-based and the correlation-based algorithms to recommend most suitable learning objects/documents for a course's units to ensure efficient learning for learners. Such an e-learning support system is capable of being embedded in any information retrieval system for surfers to ensure better and efficient Internet learning.

Ko et al (2008) proposed a helpful snippet generation method which uses a statistical query expansion approach with pseudo-relevance feedback and text summarization techniques being applied to salient sentence extraction for quality snippets. A (page/ web) snippet is a document excerpt which allows a user to know if a document is relevant without accessing it. In experiments, the proposed method proved to have much better performance than other methods including commercial Web search engines like Google and Naver.

Na et al (2007) examined usage of parsimony in query expansion and clustering algorithms effect in cluster-based retrieval. The term mismatch problem in information retrieval is critical with many techniques like query expansion, cluster-based retrieval and dimensionality reduction being developed to solve it. An empirical study on query expansion through cluster-based retrieval was undertaken. Again, query expansion and cluster-based retrieval are compared and combinations evaluated regarding retrieval performance through experiments on seven NTCIR and TREC test collections.

An effective technique to improve retrieval effectiveness, Relevance Feedback (RF) was studied in monolingual and Trans-Lingual Information Retrieval (TLIR) by He et al (2010). RF studies in TLIR were focused on Query Expansion (QE), where queries were reformulated before/after translation. RF in TLIR not only selected better query terms, but also enhanced query translation through adjusting translation probabilities and resolving out-of-vocabulary terms. This study proposes a novel relevance feedback method, Translation Enhancement (TE), using extracted translation relationships from documents to revise query terms translation probabilities and to identify extra translation alternatives to ensure that translated queries are tuned to current search. TE was studied with Pseudo-Relevance Feedback (PRF) and Interactive Relevance Feedback (IRF) and the results revealed that TE significantly improved TLIR with both relevance feedback methods, and that improvement was comparable to query expansion. Also, translation enhancement and query expansion effects were complementary, their integration further improving TLIR to be more robust for various queries.

Lin et al (2006) presented a new user relevance feedback based query expansion method to mine additional query terms. Proper query terms greatly affect document retrieval systems performance. System performance is improved by using query expansion techniques. According to user's relevance feedback, the proposed method calculates relevant terms of documents degrees of importance in the document database. Relevant terms have higher importance degrees and may become additional query terms. The proposed method uses fuzzy rules to infer additional query terms weights. Then, additional query terms weights and original query terms weights form a new query vector used for document retrieval. The proposed method increases information retrieval systems' precision and recall rates when handling document retrieval.

Mei et al (2007) proposed and studied a Poisson distribution based new family of query generation models. Many language model variants were proposed for information retrieval and most are based on multinomial distribution scoring documents on query likelihood computed on a query generation probabilistic model. It was shown that in their simplest forms, the new models family and existing multinomial models are both equal, but behave differently for smoothing methods. The Poisson model has many advantages over multinomial model. This includes accommodating per-term smoothing and ensuring more accurate background modeling. The new models variants were presented corresponding to different smoothing methods and were evaluated on four representative TREC test collections. Results revealed basic models to perform comparably, while the Poisson model outperformed multinomial model with per-term smoothing. Improved performance is possible with two-stage smoothing.

Kim et al (2011) presented novel algorithms to extract templates from many web documents generated from heterogeneous templates. World Wide Web is a useful information source. To achieve high publishing productivity, web pages in many websites are populated automatically by common content templates which provide readers access to contents through consistent structures. For machines, templates are harmful as it degrades web applications accuracy and performance due to the presence of irrelevant terms. Thus, template detection techniques gained attention recently to improve search engine performance, clustering, and web documents classification. Web documents were clustered on underlying template structures similarity in documents to ensure simultaneous extraction of templates for each cluster. A novel goodness measure was developed with approximation for clustering providing a comprehensive analysis of this algorithm. Experiments with real-life data sets confirm the algorithm's effectiveness and robustness compared to state-of-the-art template detection algorithms.

Zidi and Abed (2013) presented a generic framework for ontology-based information retrieval. Recognition of semantic information extracted from data sources and the mapping of this knowledge into ontology has been focused. Semantic indexing based on entity retrieval model has been proposed to achieve high scalability. Ontology of public transportation domain was used in order to validate these proposals. Finally, this system uses ontology mapping and real world data sources.

Xue and Yan (2012) made a research on multi agents information retrieval system based on the intelligent evolution which includes nine different modules such as user Agent, communication Agent, mining Agent, personal Agent, intelligence evolution Agent, information retrieval Agent, group Agent, and intelligence evolution filtering Agent and clustering Agent.

Based on the user history query information, current retrieval information and feedback information rectifies the judgment of the user preferences constantly, makes the returned query results.

2.5   LANGUAGE MODELLING

Language modeling approach to information retrieval was promising as it linked retrieval with language model estimation, studied extensively in applications like speech recognition. The basic idea was to estimate a language model for a document, and rank it according to query likelihood of estimated language model. Language model estimation's main problem was smoothing, which adjusts maximum likelihood estimator correct data sparseness related in accuracy. Language model smoothing and its retrieval performance influence were studied. Retrieval performance sensitivity to smoothing parameters was examined and compared to many smoothing methods on varied test collections.

Lafferty and Zhai (2001) presented an information retrieval framework combining document and query models through a probabilistic ranking function founded on Bayesian decision theory. The framework suggested operational retrieval extends language modeling approach developments to information retrieval. Each document's language model was estimated, and also a language for each query with retrieval being cast in terms of risk minimization. Query language model is exploited for user preference modeling as regards query, synonymy and word senses contexts. Recent work incorporated word translation models and methods using Markov chains were introduced on document sets for query models estimation. The Markov chain method linked algorithms from link analysis/social networks. This was evaluated on TREC collections and compared to basic language modeling and vector space models along with query expansion using Rocchio. Major improvements were seen over regular query expansion methods for strong baseline TF IDF systems, with highest improvement being for web data related short queries.

Long queries include extraneous terms hindering relevant documents retrieval. Kumaran and Carvalho(2009) suggested techniques to reduce long queries to effective short ones without extraneous terms. The work was encouraged by observing that totally lowering long TREC description queries lead to mean average precision improvements of 30%. The proposed approach necessitated converting reduction problem into a learning problem of ranking original query subsets (sub-queries) regarding their predicted quality, and selecting top sub query. Many query quality measures were described in literature as sub query representing features to train a classifier. Replacing original long query with top-ranked sub query selected by classifier results ranking lead to an average 8% improvement on test sets. Result analysis reveals that query reduction suits moderately-performing long queries, and query quality predictors small sets are compatible to rank sub-queries.

Berberich et al (2010) used a seamless approach to integrated temporal expressions in language modeling framework. Experiments reveal temporal expressions being useful in satisfying temporal information needs when their uncertainty is considered. Additional experiments/links for downloading extracted expressions and relevance assessments are seen in their technical report.

Lv and Zhai (2009) compared five representative state of the art methods to estimate query language models with pseudo feedback in ad hoc information retrieval. This included two variants of relevance language model, two variants of mixture feedback model, and divergence minimization estimation method. Experiments proved that relevance and mixture models variants outperformed others. Many heuristics were proposed intuitively related to estimation method's performance and reveal variations in heuristics implementation in varied methods to ensure an explanation of empirical observations.

Query likelihood retrieval was empirically effective for retrieval tasks. From a theoretical perspective, justification of conventional query likelihood retrieval function needs an unrealistic assumption ignoring a document's "negative query" generation, suggesting it to be a non-optimal retrieval function. Lv and Zhai (2012) attempted improving query likelihood function by reverting negative query generation. A procedure to estimate negative query generation probabilities based on maximum entropy principle proposed derived complete query likelihood retrieval containing a negative query generation component. The proposed approach bridged theoretical gaps in existing query likelihood retrieval function and also improved retrieval effectiveness without additional computational cost.

Documents temporal aspects impact relevance for certain queries. Efron and Golovchinsky (2011) built modeling of temporal information on earlier work. An extension to Query Likelihood Model including query-specific information for estimating rate parameters introduced a temporal factor in language model smoothing and query expansion through use of pseudo-relevance feedback. These extensions were evaluated by using a Twitter corpus and two newspapers article collections. Results show that compared to earlier approaches, the models are better at capturing relevance's temporal variability associated with certain topics.

Lafferty and Zhai (2003) provided a probabilistic semantics unified account underlying language modeling and information retrieval's traditional probabilistic model revealing that both procedures can be seen as equivalent probabilistically, based on different factorizations of same generative relevance model. Discussions were on how both procedures lead to varying retrieval frameworks in practice, as it involved different component models estimations.

Retrieval's language modeling approach proved to perform well empirically. Its statistical foundations are this procedure's advantage,but, feedback, as a retrieval system component was dealt with heuristically by the proposed approach. Original query was literally expanded by addition of more terms leading to expansion-based feedback creating an inconsistent original's interpretation. Zhai and Lafferty (2001) presented a principled feedback approach in language modeling where feedback was treated as updating query language model due to availability of extra evidence in feedback documents. This model-based feedback strategy fit into a language modeling approach's extension. The two different proposed approaches were updated using feedback documents based on query language model. One was based on a feedback documents generative probabilistic model, and the other on minimization of KL-divergence over feedback documents. Experiment showed that both approaches were effective, outperforming Rocchio feedback approach.

Jiang et al (2012) proposed/experimented on an adaptive browsing model. The authors wanted to present users with relevant and new results in multi-query search which discounted a document's ranking in current search due to chances that it was clearly examined by users in earlier searches in same session. A document is penalized greatly when it appears in earlier searches or when ranked in higher positions in similar searches. Documents were also ranked by combining browsing model with ad hoc search models considering users' browsing novelty in a multi-query search session. Experiments demonstrated the browsing model discounting documents found/ranked in higher positions in earlier searches, with relevant documents being shuffled to higher positions to ensure that ad hoc search performance is unaffected.

Ponte (1998) suggested use of probabilistic language models to investigate text based information retrieval and related issues. A problem was predicting text topic shifts, a topic segmentation issue. It showed that probabilistic methods can predict topic changes with regard to new event detection. Two complementary features sets were studied individually and combined into one language model. Language modeling allows a principled approach to this problem without complex semantic modeling. Next, document retrieval responding to user query was investigated. The proposed approach's advantage was collection statistics used directly in language model probabilities estimation. The proposed approach performed well on query sets and standard test collections when tested. Empirical results provided more concepts to use language models for retrieval.

Wikipedia articles were used to semantically inform query models generation by Meij and Rijke (2010) for which supervised machine learning was used to automatically link queries to Wikipedia articles/sample terms from linked articles to re-estimate query model. On a big web corpus, substantial gains regarding traditional metrics and diversity measures were noticed.

Modeling query concepts via term dependencies ensured great positive effect on retrieval performance, especially in web search, where high rank relevance was critical. Earlier work treated concepts as equally important, an assumption that usually fails with regard to longer, and more complex queries. Bendersky, et al., (2010) showed that effective existing term dependence models can be extended by assigning weights to concepts. It was proved that weighted dependence model can be trained with existing learning-to-rank techniques, even with limited training queries. The study compares effectiveness of both endogenous (collection based) and exogenous (external sources based) features to determine concept importance. To test weighted dependence model, experiments were undertaken on publicly available TREC corpora and a proprietary web corpus and results show the proposed model consistently/significantly outperformed both standard bag-of-words model and un-weighted term dependence model. It was seen that a combination of endogenous and exogenous features resulted in retrieval effectiveness.

Ostrogonac et al (2012) proposed a method of creating language models for highly inflective non-agglutinative languages. Three different types of language models were considered such as a common n-gram model, an n-gram model of lemmas and a class n-gram model. The last two types were specially designed for the Serbian language reflecting its unique grammar structure. All the language models has been trained on a collected data set which incorporates several literary styles and a great variety of domain-specific textual documents in Serbian. Language models of the three types were created for different sets of textual corpora and evaluated by perplexity values they have given on the test data.

Schulam et al (2012) presented the Source Code Statistical Language Model data analysis pattern. Statistical language model was an enabling tool for a wide array of important language technologies. Speech recognition, machine translation, and document summarization rely on statistical language models to assign probability estimates to natural language utterances or sentences. The process of building n-gram language models over software source files was described

Liu et al (2013) proposed a language model (LM) to handle the issue of poor context coverage in word sequence. In order to exploit the complementary characteristics of paraphrastic LMs and neural network LMs (NNLM), the combination between the two has been investigated. With the use of a paraphrastic multi-level LM modeling both word and phrase sequences, significant error rate reductions of 0.9% absolute (9% relative) and 0.5% absolute (5% relative) were obtained over the baseline n-gram and NNLM systems respectively, after a combination with word and phrase level NNLMs.

Zhe et al (2013) proposed the temporal kernel neural network language model, a variant of models. This model explicitly captures long-term dependencies of words with the exponential kernel, where the memory of history was decayed exponentially. In addition, several sentences with variable lengths as a mini-batch were efficiently implemented for speeding up. The results were experimental shows that the proposed model was very competitive to the recurrent neural network language model and obtains the lower perplexity of 111.6 (more than 10% reduction) than the state-of-the-art results reported in the standard Penn Treebank Corpus.

2.6   CONCEPT-BASED   APPROACHES   IN   INFORMATION RETRIEVAL

With the internet becoming faster, people tend to search and learn fragmented knowledge from it. Usually, vast documents, homepages or learning objects, are returned by powerful search engines in no specific order. Even if related, a user has to move forward/backward in the material trying to find which page to read first as the user might have limited experience in that specific domain, though a user may have domain intuition, which may in all probability be disconnected /disjointed. Hsieh, et al., (2008) suggested a learning path construction approach based on modified Term Frequency – Inverse Document Frequency (TF-IDF), Average Term Frequency – Inverse Document Frequency (ATF-IDF), and Formal Concept Analysis (FCA) algorithms. The approach first constructs a Concept Lattice with keywords from ATF-IDF collected documents to form a relationship hierarchy between all keyword represented concepts. FCA then computes mutual relationships among documents to decide on a suitable learning path.

Kashyap et al (2011) presented BioNav system, a novel search interface enabling a user to navigate many query results by organizing them through the MeSH concept hierarchy. Biomedical databases search queries like PubMed return many results of which only a small subset is user relevant. Ranking and categorization combined were suggested to alleviate information overload. The focus of this work is results categorization for biomedical databases. MeSH annotations is a natural way to organize biomedical citations which is a concept hierarchy used by PubMed. First, query results are organized into a navigation tree with each node expansion step, where BioNav reveals a small concept nodes subset, selected to reduce user navigation cost. Previous works in contrast expand hierarchy in statically, without navigation cost modelling. It is shown that selecting best concepts reveal at each node expansion is NP-complete and suggests an efficient heuristic and an optimal algorithm for smaller trees. Experiments proved that BioNav outperformed state-of-the-art categorization systems greatly regarding user navigation cost.

Tsai et al (2006) proposed an adaptive personalized ranking mechanism to recommend SCORM-compliant learning objects from internet repositories. Digital courses have many learning units/learning objects, creating many learning objects according to SCORM standard. In the future, a huge number of SCORM-compliant learning objects will be published/distributed across the net. Facing this, learners will find it very hard to select suitable learning objects. The proposed mechanism uses preference-based and neighbour-interest-based approaches to rank the relevance degree of learning objects for a user. Through this, a tutoring system provides suitable learning objects easily for active learners.

Hubscher et al (2010) proposed a method allowing instructors to combine a general criterion and a context-specific preference flexible set to describe group types preferred. Group projects are important in many courses. This enables instructors to allow students to form own groups or assign them to one to increase group effectiveness. Computational tools supporting student's assignments in class projects use general criterion, for instance, maximizing group member's diversity. The instructor needs to consider frequently additional context-specific criteria/preferences which force him to figure out student's assignments manually instead of through software. This task, though difficult and time consuming, results in suboptimal assignments. The proposed heuristic Tabu Search algorithm locates solutions that satisfy many preferences.

A current Web search problem is short and ambiguous search queries which are insufficient to specify precise user needs. To overcome this, search engines suggest terms semantically related to submitted queries to enable users to choose from suggestions that which reflects their information needs. Leung, et al., (2008) introduced an effective approach to capture user's conceptual preferences to provide personalized query suggestions. This is achieved through two new strategies. First, online techniques that extract concepts from the web-snippets of the search result returned from a query are organized and concepts identify related queries for a specific query. Second, a new two phase personalized agglomerative clustering algorithm capable of generating personalized query clusters is proposed. No earlier work has addressed personalization for query suggestions. A Google middleware was developed to evaluate the technique's effectiveness, and this was done through collecting click through data for evaluation. Experiments showed this approach to have better precision and recall than current query clustering methods.

Iosif et al (2010) presented Web-based metrics to compute words' and terms semantic similarity and were compared with state of the art techniques. From the fundamental assumption that context similarity implies meaning similarity, relevant Web documents were downloaded through a Web search engine and contextual information of words of interest compared (context-based similarity metrics). The proposed algorithms work automatically, without human-annotated knowledge resources, e.g., ontology. It can be generalized /applied to differing languages. Charles-Miller data set and a medical term data set evaluated context based metrics revealing that context-based similarity metrics greatly outperformed co-occurrence-based metrics regarding human judgment correlation for both tasks. Additionally, the proposed unsupervised context-based similarity computation algorithms are competitive with state-of-the-art supervised semantic similarity algorithms using language-specific knowledge resources. Context-based metrics had correlation scores of up to 0.88 and 0.74 for Charles-Miller and medical data sets, respectively. The stop word filtering effect is investigated for word/term similarity computation. Performance of context-based term similarity metrics is evaluated as a web documents function for various feature weighting schemes.

Lee et al (2006) presented a semantic-aware learning object retrieval based ontological approach with two novel features: an automatic ontology-based query expansion algorithm to infer and aggregate user intentions based on original short query, and an "ambiguity removal" procedure to correct incorrect user queries. This approach can be embedded in other LOM-based search mechanisms to ensure semantic-aware learning object retrieval. The proposed approach - focused on digital learning material, contrasting other traditional keyword-based search technologies has demonstrated experimentally, greatly improved retrieval precision and recall rate.

Dilshener(2012) proposed an improved information retrieval based on the concept location by the contextual relationship. The existing technique was based on information retrieval (IR) which provides an adequate solution. Such techniques usually consider the conceptual relations based on lexical similarities during concept mapping. Proposed work uses the domain specific ontological relations during concept mapping and location activities when implementing business requirements.

Moon and Yoon (2013) presented a keyword base concept model for information retrieval. A keyword-based concept network was a method with the application of ontology. However, the proposed model has been added by association information between keyword concepts as a method for a user's efficient information retrieval. Also this concept network contains a keyword centered concept network, expert-group-recommended field concept network, and process concept network in it.

Shan et al (2012) proposed a meta search engine personalized mechanism which was based on ontology with the use of the Agent technology which mine the user behavior of characteristics with Agent for information retrieval by combining ontology technology set up and update the user general view which thereby reflects the user current interest and to the user's interest to the renewal of the dynamic. Based on ontology users, the user's query scene reasoning and filter search has been made. The results makes the search results to meet user needs, has the personalized.

Ta and Thi (2012) proposed an algorithm for improving the formal concept analysis to construct the ontology domain. With different purposes, both Domain Ontology and Formal Concept Analysis (FCA) were models used to present modeling concepts. FCA uses a lattice in mathematics to present concepts based on objects and attributes, where domain Ontology also presents the concepts and was used in various areas such as biology, information retrieval, information extraction, etc. hence to build Domain Ontology based on FCA in order to support the information extraction task on a specified domain has been proposed.

CHAPTER 3

DYNAMIC NOMINAL LANGUAGE MODEL FOR INFORMATION RETRIEVAL

3.1 INTRODUCTION

Information Retrieval (IR) models produce ranking functions which assign scores to documents regarding a given query and this consists of two tasks: The task representing documents and query and the task which computes each document rank. IR systems build index terms to index and retrieve documents. Usually most index terms are any keyword which appears in text document collections. Most users have no opinion/training in query formation to retrieve results. To retrieve answers to a query, IR system predicts documents users find relevant/irrelevant. Predicting function is a ranking algorithm to ensure ordering of retrieved documents.

Language modelling approach to retrieval performs well. An advantage of this new approach is its statistical foundation. This approach to text retrieval was introduced by Ponte and Croft (1998) and later explored by (Song et al 1999; Allan et al 2002; Balog et al 2009). Language modelling approach's simplicity and effectiveness with the fact that it leverages statistical methods developed in speech recognition and other areas ensures its attraction in developing new text retrieval methodology.

3.2   LANGUAGE MODELLING IN IR

Simple language models incorporate document and collection statistics systematically than Term Frequency–Inverse Document Frequency (tf.idf) based techniques Language models and classical models using tf.idf work well, but further improvements require more techniques in addition to language modelling. Language modelling approach is shared with classical probabilistic approaches to IR, in that probabilistic modelling is taken as the primary scientific tool. Currently, this is a promising framework to advance information retrieval to meet challenges from diverse data sources/advanced retrieval tasks.

Language Model defines documents probability distribution using them to predict likelihood of query terms observation. Language model has been defined for all documents and it is used to inquire about chances of query generation. Some commonly used models are as:

3.2.1   Language Model based on Markov process:

Language model uses Markov process to assign occurrence probability to a word sequence 'S' as follows

$$P_n(S) = \prod_{i=1}^{r} P(K_i | K_{i-1}, K_{i-2} \dots K_{i-(n-1)}) \qquad (3.1)$$

n   -   order of the Markov process

if n=1,   then the model is called Unigram model.

3.2.2   Language Model based on Bernoulli process:

If index terms independence is assumed, then $P(q|M_j)$ has been computed using Multi-variable Bernoulli process.

$$P_n(K_i|M_j) = \prod_{k_i \in \Lambda} \cdot \prod_{\notin q} P(K_i|M_j) \qquad (3.2)$$

The simple estimate of term probabilities

$$P(K_i|M_j) = \frac{f_{i,j}}{\sum_i f_{i,j}} \qquad (3.3)$$

3.2.3　Language Model based on Multi-nominal process

If terms' being independent among them is assumed, probability scoring function is defined as

$$P(q|M_j) = \prod_{K \in q} P(K_i|M_j) \qquad (3.4)$$

By taking the log on both sides

$$\text{Log } P(q|M_j) = \sum_{K_i \in q} Log P(K_i|M_j) \qquad (3.5)$$

$$= \sum_{K_i \in \Lambda \cdot} \cdot \sum_{\notin \Lambda d_j} Log P(K_i|M_j) \qquad (3.6)$$

3.2.4　Language model based on Poisson Distribution

On the Poisson setup,

$$P(d\,|\,\text{R}) = \prod_{K_i \in q} \frac{e^{-\lambda}\lambda^{d_i}}{d\,!} \qquad (3.7)$$

$$P(d\,|\neg \text{R}) = \prod_{K_i \in q} \frac{e^{-\mu_i}\mu_i^{d_i}}{d\,!} \qquad (3.8)$$

The similarity meantime is derived as

$$Sim(d,q) = O(R \mid d) = \frac{P(R \mid d)}{P(\neg R \mid d)}$$

$$Sim(d,q) = \sum_{Ki \in q} d \log \lambda - \qquad \mu_i \qquad (3.9)$$

The maximum likelihood estimation for the Poisson distribution

$$\mu_i = \frac{1}{n} \sum_{i=1}^{n} d_i \qquad (3.10)$$

For n documents with values d_i as word frequencies

3.2.5 Smoothing

Using estimate smoothing is necessary to avoid over-fitting (believing information given by small observed sample). Smoothing estimates and accounts for unseen terms in relevant/non-relevant documents.

3.2.6 Query Likelihood Model

Query likelihood model is based on query generation probability in document language model

$$Score(Q, D) = \prod_{i=1}^{n} P(q_i \mid \theta_D) \qquad (3.11)$$

q_i denotes i^{th} query term.

Using linear interpolation smoothing query likelihood model sources documents as

$$Score(Q;D) = \prod_{i=1}^{n} \cdots \quad \quad + \quad - \lambda, \quad \theta_c) \qquad (3.12)$$

where θ_c denotes the collection language model and λ denotes the mining co-efficient.

3.3   QUERY LIKELIHOOD RETRIEVAL METHOD

The query likelihood retrieval method (Ponte et al 1998) enjoyed success in many retrieval tasks (Zhai et al 2001). It assumes that a query is a sample from a language model: given a query Q and a document D, the likelihood of "generating" query Q with a model estimated based on document D is assumed. Documents based on likelihood of generating query are assumed.

Though query likelihood performed well, its theoretical foundation (Robertson et al 2001;Jones et al 2001) was criticised. Lafferty and Zhai (2002) proved that under certain assumptions, query likelihood retrieval method was justified based on probability ranking principle(Robertson et al 1977) and being regarded as probabilistic retrieval models foundation.

In query likelihood retrieval (Ponte et al 1998), given a query Q and a document D, the likelihood of "generating"query Q with a model $\theta_D$estimated based on document$D$, is computed and then the document, based on its query likelihood is ranked:

$$Score(D,Q) = p(Q | \theta_D) \qquad (3.13)$$

The query generation is based on any language model(Miller et al 1999; Zhai et al 2001; Metzler et al 2004; Mei et al 2007; Tsagkias et al 2011). Till date, using a multinomial distribution (Miller et al 1999; Zhai et al 2001) for θ_D was popular and successful. With multinomial distribution, query likelihood is

$$p(Q|\theta_D) = \prod_w \left(\theta_D \right)^{c(w,Q)} \qquad (3.14)$$

where $c\ (w,Q)$ is count of term w in query Q. According to maximum likelihood estimator, the following estimation of document language model θ_D for multinomial model is ready:

$$p_{ml}(w|\theta_D) = \frac{c(w,D)}{|D|} \qquad (3.15)$$

where $c\ (w,D)$ indicates frequency of w in document D, and $|D|$ is document length. θ_D needs smoothing to offset zero-probability problem, with an effective method being the Dirichlet prior smoothing (Zhai, et al., 2001):

$$p(w|\theta_D) = \frac{|D|}{|D|+} p_{ml}(w|D) + \frac{\mu}{|D|+\mu} p(w|C) \qquad (3.16)$$

Here μ is the smoothing parameter (Dirichlet prior), and $p(w|C)$ is the collection language model which is estimated as

$$p(w|C) = \frac{c(w,C)}{\sum_w c(w',C)} \qquad (3.7)$$

where $c(w,C)$ indicates the count of term w in the whole collection C.

Query likelihood scoring function ranks documents using following formula (Zhai et al 2001):

$$\log p(Q|\theta_D) \overset{rank}{=} \sum_{w\in Q\cap D} \left(\right) + |Q| \log \frac{\mu}{|D|+\mu} \qquad (3.18)$$

where $|Q|$ represents query length.

3.3.1   Query Reformulation and Expansion

To fine-tune/revise the query, two techniques consider relevant feedback

(i)   Query expansion adding new query terms to query from high relevant document

(ii)   Term Reweighting: This increases terms weight in relevant documents and decreases terms weight those irrelevant.

3.3.2   Query Reformulation Algorithm

Revise Query vectors using vector Algebra:

(i)   Add vectors for relevant documents to query vector.

(ii)   Subtract vectors for irrelevant document from query vector.

This process adds positive/negative weighted terms to query & reweights initial query terms.

3.4   NOMINAL LANGUAGE MODEL (NLM)

Nominal Language Model (NLM) based language modelling goes with part of speech of a given query's literal language, constituting factors with noun and adjectives. Informational query attempts to capture a document with data, relevant to analysis area. NLM based Information Retrieval process is an efficient method to extract relevant documents. Language modelling is processed with natural language processing methods.

3.5 RETRIEVAL METRICS - PRECISION AND RECALL

Precision and Recall metrics evaluate a set of un-ranked results and consider differences between documents set retrieved for a query and documents set relevant to a user's need. Trade-off between Precision and Recall can also be user specific. Some users care about precision/recall, without asking users, how a search engine can guess whether a specific user cares more about precision than recall or vice versa.

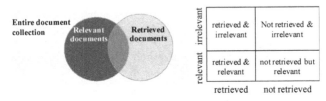

$$recall = \frac{Number\ of\ relevant\ documents\ retrieved}{Total\ number\ of\ relevant\ documents}$$

$$precision = \frac{Number\ of\ relevant\ documents\ retrieved}{Total\ number\ of\ documents\ retrieved}$$

Figure 3.1 Retrieval metrics

If Information request I and its set R of relevant documents, answers I set A, then precision and recall measures are as follows. Precision is retrieved documents fraction (A) relevant to

$$\Pr ecision = P = \frac{|R \cap A|}{|A|} \quad (3.19)$$

Recall is relevant documents(R) fraction determined

$$\operatorname{Re} call = r = \frac{|R \cap A|}{|R|} \quad (3.20)$$

3.6 FLOW CHART OF THE PROPOSED METHODOLOGY

Flow chart of the proposed technique is shown in Figure 3.2.

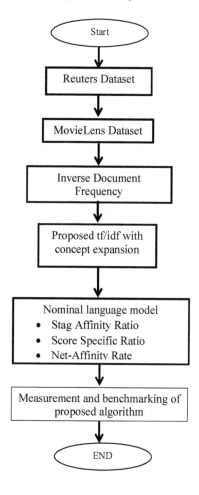

Figure 3.2 Flowchart of the Proposed Methodology

The following sections details the various techniques used in the proposed method.

3.6.1 Datasets

The different types of Dataset include:

3.6.1.1 Reuters-21578 Dataset

The Reuters-21578 Text Categorization Test Collection is a standard text categorization benchmark having 21578 Reuters news documents from 1987, all labelled manually. Labels are of five different categories like 'people', 'places' and 'topics'. Total categories are 672 with many occurring very rarely. The Reuters-21578 data set is commonly used for newswire stories categorization into hand-labelled topics. Each news story is hand-labelled with some topic labels like "corn", "wheat" and "corporate acquisitions". Some topics overlap and hence belong to more than one category. The 12902 articles from "ModApte" split of the data five were used and, to stay comparable with previous studies, top ten most frequent topics were considered. Reuter's collection is distributed in 22 files beginning with a document type declaration:

<DOCTYPElewis SYSTEM "lewis.dtd">

Each article starts with an "open tag" of the form

<REUTERS TOPICS=?? LEWISSPLIT=?? CGISPLIT=?? OLDID=?? NEWID=??>

where the ?? are filled appropriately. Each article ends with the form's "close tag.":

</REUTERS>

Each REUTERS tag specifies values of five attributes: TOP-ICS, LEWISSPLIT, CGISPLIT, OLDID, and NEWID which identify documents and document groups. Attribute values determine how documents are divided into training and test sets. The experiments in this work used modified Apte split, most used in literature.

Each document represents a stemmed, TF-IDF weighted word frequency vector with each vector having unit modulus. A common words stop list was used with words occurring in less than three documents being ignored.

3.6.1.2   MovieLens dataset

Group Lens Research (http://www.grouplens.org/node/73) gives many collections of movie ratings data gathered from users of MovieLens in late 1990s and early 2000s. Data provides movie ratings, movie metadata (genres/year), and users demographic data (age, zip code, gender, occupation). The second dataset is provided by Movie-Lens research project, a web–based movie recommender system that began in 1997 and includes 943 users, 1,682 movies and has 100,000 transactions totally. Ratings are based on a 1 to 5 scale. The archive has many files, with a list of movie IDs and titles, and u. data, containing actual ratings in the following format:

196 242 3   881250949

186 302 3   891717742

22   377 1   878887116

244 51   2   880606923

166 346 1   886397596

298 474 4   884182806

3.6.2 Inverse Document Frequency (IDF)

Inverse Document Frequency (IDF) is a numerical statistic reflecting the importance of a word to a document in a collection/corpus, often used as a weighting factor in information retrieval/text mining. IDF value increases in proportion to the many times a word appears in the document, and offset by the word's frequency in the corpus. This helps control the fact that some words are more common than others. IDF weighting scheme variations are used by search engines as a central tool in scoring/ranking a document's relevance regarding a user query. IDF is successfully used to filter stop-words in various fields like text summarization/classification. The latter is a semi-supervised, machine learning task which automatically assigns a document to a set of pre-defined categories based on textual content and extracted features.

Inverse Document Frequency (IDF) is a measure of word's importance and usually appears in many heuristic measures in information retrieval. Till now IDF has been a heuristic, a popular measure of a word's importance and defined as the logarithm of the ratio of documents number having a given word. This ensures that rare words have high IDF and common words like "the" have low IDF which measures a word's ability to discriminate between documents. Text Classification assigns a text document to a pre-defined class set automatically, through machine learning. Classification is on the basis of significant words/key-features of a text document. As classes are pre-defined it becomes a supervised machine learning task.

The term document frequency is computed as follows for a set of documents x and a set of terms a. Each document is modelled as a vector v in the a dimensional space R^a. The term frequency denoted by $freq(x,a)$, expresses the number of occurrence of the term a in document x. The term-frequency matrix $TF(x,a)$ measures term association a with regard to a given document x. $TF(x,a)$ is assigned zero when the document has no term and $TF(x,a)=1$ when term a occurs in the document x or uses a relative term frequency which is **term frequency** as against the total occurrences of all document terms. Frequency is generally normalized by (Liu, et al., 2007):

$$TF(x,a) = \begin{cases} 0 & freq(\ )=0 \\ 1+ \ (+\log(freq(x,a))) & otherwise \end{cases}$$

(3.21)

Document/term	t 1	t 2	t 3	t 4	t 5	t 6	t 7
d 1	0	5	12	6	0	2	0
d 2	4	7	0	19	0	1	24
d 3	12	15	4	0	15	12	17
d 4	23	4	9	3	12	3	0
d 5	0	3	7	2	9	9	7

Figure 3.3   Term frequency matrix showing frequency of terms per document

IDF represents scaling factor. When a term a occurs frequently in many documents, its importance is then scaled down because of its lowered discriminative power. The $IDF(a)$ is defined as follows:

$$IDF(a) = \log \frac{1+|x|}{x_a}$$

(3.22)

x_a is the set of documents containing term a.

73

TF-IDF usually uses text categorisation metric having two scores, term frequency and inverse document frequency. Term frequency is counting the times a term occurs in a document, while inverse document-frequency is attained by dividing total documents by documents where a specific word appears repeatedly. The multiplication of values results in a high score for frequently occurring words in limited documents. A low score is meant for terms appearing frequently in all documents.

Similar documents will have same relative term frequencies measured among a document set or between document and query. Cosine measure helps to locate similarity between documents. The cosine measure is given by:

$$sim(v_1, v_2) = \frac{v_1.v_2}{|v_1||v_2|}$$

(3.23)

where v_1 and v_2 are two document vectors, $v_1.v_2$ defined as $\sum_{i=1}^{a} v_{1i}v_{2i}$ and $|v_1| = \sqrt{v_1.v_1}$.

(3.24)

Figure 3.4 illustrates the relation between df_t and idf_t for a total of million documents.

Term	df_t	idf_t
brilliant	100	4
good	1000	3
under	10000	2
with	100000	1
the, movie	1000000	0

Figure 3.4   Relation between the df_t and idf_t for a total of million documents

3.6.3   Proposed tf/idf with Concept Expansion

A term/phrase can have many meanings, while a domain specific concept is unambiguous. It is useful to use the domain specific concepts in documents than terms to retrieve documents from a specific domain. Hence, the list of concepts in documents is extracted and a list of concepts annotates them. Too ensure this, the meaning of a term needs to be disambiguated to identify the concept it refers to. More than one term may refer to the same concept in some cases. Then concept frequency will include frequencies of the concept's synonymous terms in the document (Roy et al 2008).

This rarely occurs in isolation. When a concept is important for a document, it usually has other related concepts. For example, 'charge' has at least two distinct meanings: electric charge and financial charge. When a document speaks about electric charge, the document will have other terms like current, electricity, etc. while in the case of financial charge; document will have terms like payment, amount, etc. The idea is to score a concept by looking at it and references to related concepts.

A list of terms and frequencies exists for each document. How each term in document is mapped to its corresponding concept and how each concept's significance is estimated regarding the current document are discussed. An associated set of concepts for each term is obtained from ontology. A term maps to one or more concepts. As explained earlier the term 'charge' can map to electric charge, financial charge or criminal charge. Out of mapped concepts, the most appropriate concept for a specific domain should be located. Related concepts occurrences are looked into for this. Captured inter-concept relationship in ontology is used.

Figure 3.5 reveals a portion of concept graph in the ontology's physics domain (Roy et al 2010). A concept becomes significant when the document has many related concepts of that particular term. The proposed algorithm uses document terms with their frequency as input returning a concepts list with their significance regarding the document.

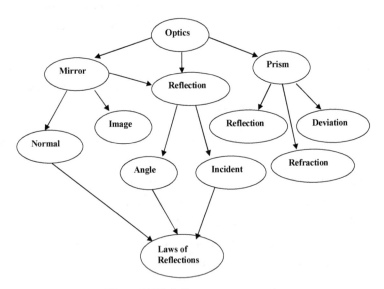

Figure 3.5 Relation among concepts

The algorithm works as follows. For each term t_i in the term list of a document D, the associated concepts c_{ij} are obtained from the ontology. Let the impact of each associated concept c_{ij} be c_{ij} _impact_. The impact c_{ij} _impact_ is initially taken as the normalized frequency of the term t_i i.e. t_i. _frequency_. For each associated concept c_{ij}, the presence of the related concepts rc_p in the document is taken into account. The impact of the associated concept c_{ij} is then incremented by α*normalized term frequency for the occurrences of the terms t_p corresponding to the concept rc_p.

where α is the weight given to the related concepts. In this study, the value given is $\alpha = \frac{1}{2}$.

For a particular term, a concept with maximum significance value is selected.

The algorithm is outlined below:

Algorithm 1: Identification of Concept and its significance

Input: t_1, t_2, .., t_n is the list of domain terms in the document D;

$t_i.frequency$ is the normalized frequency of domain term t_i ;

num is the total number of tokens in the document D

Output: list of concepts c_1, c_2, ... c_m and their impact $c_i.impact$

for $i \leftarrow 1$ *to n*

{

$t_i.frequency \leftarrow t_i.frequency / num$

}

for $i \leftarrow 1$ *to n*

{

$t_i.concepts \leftarrow \{c_{i1}.. \, c_{ij}.c_{ik}\}$

$c_{ij}.impact \leftarrow t_i.frequency$

}

for $i \leftarrow 1$ *to n*

{

for $j \leftarrow 1$ *to k*

{

find the related concept $src_p.of\, c_{ij}\,(rc_p.$'s corresponding term $tp)$ in D

if t_p occurs in D

$c_{ij}.impact \leftarrow$ $+$ $\times$ $= 1/2$

}

}

    for $i \leftarrow 1$ *to* n

{

if $x.impact > threshold$

return x

else

return null

}

The algorithm returns the list of concepts and their impact scores.

Word Net is a lingual database for English, the link language and is termed as an abounding lexical database for English constituting groups of nouns, verbs, adjectives and adverbs called synsets, contrived on conceptual semantic and lingual relations. A corpus with proposed concept expansion using Word Net is formed.

3.6.4 Dynamic Nominal Language Model (DNLM)

In this proposal, NLM is assembled with rate specifications and ratio calculations through use of probabilistic terms involving comparing query terms occurrence with data store using conditional probability theorem.

3.6.4 Dynamic Nominal Language Model (DNLM)

In this proposal, NLM is assembled with rate specifications and ratio calculations through use of probabilistic terms involving comparing query terms occurrence with data store using conditional probability theorem.

3.6.4.1 Stag Affinity Ratio

Query expansion follows calculation of stag affinity ratio. Conditional probability is applied for query term with each document term being subjected to many occurrences. This proposal conjugates semantic methods and Language Model Techniques. This conjugative IR method audits single word's clear meanings in the query leading to results with accuracy. P (Q|T), called LM Coefficient (γ) determines each term's occurrence number in each document. LM coefficient is evaluated by,

$$P(Q|T_i) = \frac{a+b}{a}$$

(3.25)

where 'i' denotes terms number, 'a' represents each term's co-occurrence number and 'b' stands on denoting the term. Similarly, each term's weight corresponding to WordNet affinity is calculated and noted as 'w'.

Stag affinity rate (δ) is the product of individual word weight in the document and occurrences number of each term of a given query, termed as LM coefficient here.

$$\delta_k = \sum_{j=1}^{m} \log \left\{ \prod_{i=1}^{n} [(\gamma_i, w_i)_j] \right\}$$

(3.26)

where 'i' varies from $1 \le i \le n$, stands for query terms, 'j' ranges $1 \le j \le m$, denotes terms number in each document and 'k' represents documents number.

The affinity rate for each word is calculated and finally iterated for all words in the document. A document is related to query regarding similarity, occurrence and relationship. To approximate stag affinity rate, its log value is first determined, thus making an effective evaluation criteria reducing fluctuations over high values determined by stag affinity rate. So, there is a possibility of participation and non-participation terms in user query regarding WordNet, a lexical English database. To improve the proposed algorithm's consistency based on IR, association participation and non-participation rate terms of WordNet regarding user query is evaluated. Participation terms go with remaining probabilistic measurements there being a necessity to determine non-participating terms ratio of each document's query. Non-Participating terms count evaluation reduces effects on accurate results. Association between non-participation and participation terms are evaluated through application of Kendal Coefficient. Stag affinity rate for non-participation terms will be 0. When the Kendal coefficient equation results are negative, it reveals higher non-participation terms in user query. Association between participation and non-participation word is termed elusion phrase ratio (τ). Kendal coefficient is a non-parametric statistic with concordance.

Generally, Kendal coefficient ranges from 0 to 1 and value assumed regarding probabilistic distribution values. Kendal's coefficient elusion phrase ratio is given by,

$$\text{Elusion Phrase Ratio } (\tau_k) = \left(\frac{P\text{-}NP}{P + NP}\right)\Big/_\alpha \qquad (3.27)$$

where P represents participation terms and NP represents non-participation term regarding WordNet and α here is an arbitrary constant implying on range between $0 \leq \alpha \leq 1$. This calculation is biased for query terms accuracy determination.

3.6.4.2 Score Specific Ratio

Dependency between LM Coefficient and term weights is applied to correlation statistics to compute score specific ratio (ρ) value. Computation is through application of Pearson correlation coefficient to participating items numbers. Determination of (μ) is given as,

$$\text{Score Specific Ratio} = \rho_{(w,y)}$$

where, correlation coefficient between weight and LM coefficient $\rho_{(w,y)}$ is conferred as,

$$\rho_{(w,y)_k} = \frac{\sum_{i=1}^{n}\left(w_i - \bar{w}\right)\left(y_i - \bar{y}\right)}{\sqrt{\sum_{i=1}^{n}\left(w_i - \bar{w}\right)^2 \sum_{i=1}^{n}\left(y_i - \bar{y}\right)^2}} \tag{3.28}$$

The correlation calculation defines dependence statistical relationship between measured weight and LM coefficient value. Correlation coefficient imposes dependency degree between given terms against document. The score specific ratio produces a tedious value. Mean correlation value is obtained from ρ_k of terms in a given query individually being applied for net-affinity rate evaluation. It ensures unvarying correlation value for more estimates. Thus, Monotonousness is evaluated by this correlation calculation. Determination of score specific ratio is an important part of affinity based Nominal Language Model, specifying correlation between weight of words in the document set and the Language Model Coefficient for excerpting number of words occurrences of user query against document set.

3.6.4.3 Net-Affinity Rate

Net-affinity rate is calculated through use of stag affinity rate, calculated to determine query terms similarity rate regarding WordNet, score specific ratio specifying correlation between word weight and LM coefficient and elusion phrase ratio for determining participation and non-participation terms association.

Net-affinity rate is described further by ratio of stag affinity rate and score specific ratio with destruction of elusion phrase ratio, mentioned (τ).

$$\sigma^r_{k=1} = \left[\frac{\delta_k}{\rho_k}\right] \cdot \tau_k \tag{3.29}$$

where 'k' represents the document sets and varies as $0 \leq k \leq r$.

Net-Affinity Rate finds similarity ratio for terms in user query with classifier having all relevant documents. The results sum up similarity ratio for all terms in query with entire document set. Terminal calculation of the proposed method is Net-affinity rate evaluation, summarizing all similarities and correlates results. The outcome is documents with greater accuracy relevant to user query which are ranked, based on scores for efficient result display.

The concept extraction module identifies each document's concept; this is being done through an ontology collection. Terms are matched to the ontology's concepts, synonyms, metonyms and hyponyms.Concept weight aka semantic weights are estimated through the concept and its element count. A semantic cube is constructed using concepts and semantic weight. The latter is calculated for a term, the weight being calculated on the number of occurrences. It is then multiplied with 100% weight for a concept. Semantic weights of other relations are calculated by equation

$$Z = \begin{cases} \text{Re lationship name} & \text{Semantic weight calculation} \\ \text{Synonym} & \text{Term count} * \dfrac{60}{100} \\ \text{Meronym} & \text{Term count} * \dfrac{40}{100} \\ \text{Hypernym} & \text{Term count} * \dfrac{20}{100} \end{cases}$$

Association rule is finally applied to words group to find a frequent item set. Agrawal, et al.,(1993) provided an association rule mining statement for transaction databases. Let I ={i1, i2, . . . ,im} be the universe of items. A set X of items is an itemset. A transaction t =(tid ,X) is a tuple where tid is a unique transaction ID and X an itemset. A transaction database D is a transactions set. The count of an item set X in D, denoted by count(X), is the number of transactions in D containing X. The support of an itemset X in D, denoted by 25 supp(X), is transactions proportion in D containing X. The rule X ->Y holds in the transaction set D with confidence c wherec = conf(X->Y) and conf(X->Y) = supp(XY)/supp(X), where supp(XY) denotes support of itemsX and Y occurring together. Association rule mining aims to retrieve all rules of the formX- >Y where supp(XY) > s and conf(X->Y) >c, with s and c being Learner-supplied thresholds on minimum support and minimum confidence respectively (Agrawal, et al.,1993). Association rules are built by locating frequent itemsetshaving a support greater than defined threshold. Based on this, rules with a minimum confidence are selected.

3.7   EXPERIMENTAL SETUP AND RESULTS

Reuters dataset evaluates the proposed methods. Query expansion involves evaluation of user query with regard to information retrieval methodologies. Query expansion process is followed by calculations with nominal language modelling. NLM involves determination of Net-affinity rate comparing user query with WordNet data store through calculations with conditional probability of conceits. WordNetincludes English language related data which provides user queries. It constitutes synsets which define short, common descriptions and store various semantic correlations between synonym sets. Elusion phrase ratio is then calculated to find the query's non participation terms against WordNet data store. The weight of each user query is determined on its occurrences/importance, with score ratio being calculated with evaluated weight and the language model coefficient. Association rules are found.

Precision values for various techniques for MovieLens dataset and Reuters dataset are evaluated. The techniques used were tdf.idf, Language modelling using query likelihood, proposed concept expansion and proposed DNLM. The experimental results for MovieLens dataset for precision and F measure are tabulated in Table 3.1 and Table 3.2 respectively. Figure 3.6 and 3.7 show the same.

Table 3.1Precision values for various techniques for MovieLens dataset

Recall	TDF-IDF	Concept expansion	Language modelling using Query likelihood	DNLM
0.01	0.6912	0.7321	0.7128	0.793
0.1	0.633	0.6912	0.6732	0.7487
0.2	0.614	0.625	0.632	0.677
0.3	0.612	0.618	0.606	0.6694
0.4	0.5623	0.593	0.572	0.6423
0.5	0.541	0.572	0.558	0.6196
0.6	0.492	0.568	0.542	0.6153
0.7	0.4602	0.534	0.521	0.5784
0.8	0.421	0.501	0.49	0.5427
0.9	0.4101	0.464	0.432	0.5026
1	0.2308	0.3911	0.362	0.321

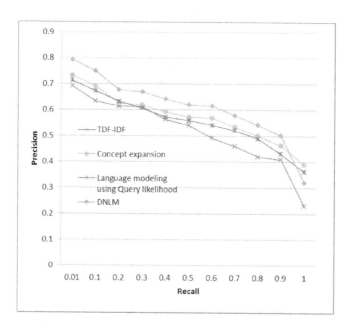

Figure 3.6 Precision values for various techniques for MovieLens dataset

From the Figure 3.6 it is seen that precision values for DNLM is higher than the precision values for all the other techniques. The precision values for DNLM is higher than the precision values for tdf.idf by 14.7% when recall is 0.01 and 22.5% when recall is 0.9. DNLM performs better than concept expansion by 8.3% when recall is 0.01 and 0.9. Similarly for Language modelling using query likelihood, DNLM performs better by 11 % when recall is 0.01 and 16% when recall is 0.09.

Table 3.2 Average F measure values for various techniques for MovieLens dataset

	TDF-IDF	Concept expansion	Language modelling using Query likelihood	DNLM
F measure	0.507972	0.533996243	0.526405368	0.550098

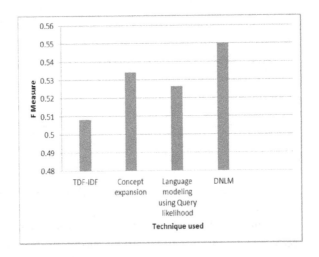

Figure 3.7 Average F measure values for various techniques for MovieLens dataset

From the Figure 3.7 it is seen that average f measure values for DNLM is higher than the average f measure values for all the other techniques. The average f measure values for DNLM is higher than the average f measure values for tdf.idf by 8%, concept expansion by 3% and Language modelling using query likelihood by 4.5 %.

The experimental results for Reuters-21758 dataset for precision and F measure are tabulated in Table 3.3 and Table 3.4 respectively. Figure 3.8 and 3.9 show the same.

Table 3.3   Precision values for various techniques for Reuters-21758 dataset

Recall	TDF-IDF	Concept expansion	Language modelling using Query likelihood	DNLM
0.01	0.7646	0.8099	0.7885	0.8772
0.1	0.7002	0.7646	0.7447	0.8282
0.2	0.6792	0.6914	0.6991	0.7489
0.3	0.677	0.6836	0.6704	0.7405
0.4	0.622	0.656	0.6328	0.7105
0.5	0.5985	0.6328	0.6173	0.6854
0.6	0.5443	0.6283	0.5996	0.6807
0.7	0.5091	0.5907	0.5763	0.6398
0.8	0.4657	0.5542	0.542	0.6003
0.9	0.4537	0.5133	0.4779	0.556
1	0.2553	0.4326	0.4004	0.3551

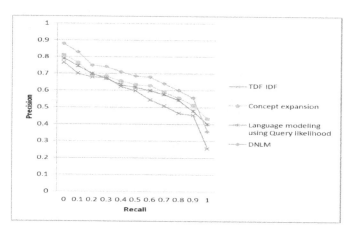

Figure 3.8   Precision values for various techniques for Reuters-21758 dataset

The Figure 3.8 shows the relationship between precision and recall and it is seen that precision values for DNLM is higher when compared with the precision values for all the other techniques. The precision values for DNLM is higher than the precision values for tdf.idf by 14.7% when recall is 0.01and 22.5% when recall is 0.9. DNLM performs better than concept expansion by 8.3% when recall is 0.01and 0.9. Similarly for Language modelling using query likelihood, DNLM performs better by 11 % when recall is 0.01 and 16% when recall is 0.09. Increasing recall conceivably increases the quality of the results with more relevant documents.

Table 3.4   Average F measure values for various techniques for Reuters-21758 dataset

	TDF-IDF	Concept expansion	Language modelling using Query likelihood	DNLM
F measure	0.532699	0.558495	0.550983	0.574389

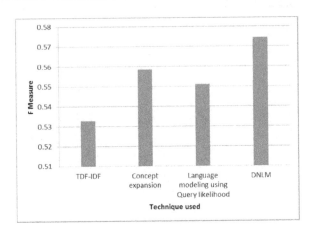

Figure 3.9   Average F measure values for various techniques for Reuters-21758 dataset

It is apparent from the above pictorial representation that the proposed methodology produces higher average f measure than the existing tdf.idf method, concept expansion and Language modelling using Query likelihood. The average f measure values for DNLM is higher than the average f measure values for tdf.idf by 7.8%, concept expansion by 2.8 %, and Language modelling using query likelihood by 4.2%.

3.8   CONCLUSION

This work proposes a method for Information Retrieval based on Nominal Language Model supporting e-learning environments. A term/phrase has multiple meanings, while a domain specific concept can be unambiguous. It is useful and better to use documents domain specific concepts than retrieving documents terms which belong to a specific domain. Hence, list of concepts present in documents are extracted and annotated with the concepts lists. NLM based approach includes lexical resources of natural language processing where the process moves through data extraction with given query. Methods of conditional probability theorem were used to determine Affinity rates to ensure that this approach was persuasive. Experiments showed that proposed DNLM method achieved better precision compared to traditional tdf.idf and Language modelling using Query likelihood.

CHAPTER 4

CLUSTER BASED FEATURE SELECTION USING HYBRID PARTICLE SWARM OPTIMIZATION

4.1 INTRODUCTION

Feature selection selects an original features subset. Feature subsets optimality is measured through an evaluation criterion. As domain dimensionality expands, number of N features increases. It is intractable to locate an optimal feature subset (Kohavi et al 1997) and feature selection related problems are NP-hard (Blum et al 1992). Feature selection has four basic steps including subset generation, subset evaluation, stopping criterion, and result validation (Dash et al 1997). Subset generation is a search procedure (Langley et al 1994; Liu et al 1998) to evaluate candidate feature subsets based on a specific search strategy. A candidate subset is evaluated/compared to one previous best based on certain evaluation criteria. When a new subset is better, it replaces the previous one of the same quality. Subset generation and evaluation are repeated till a specific stopping criterion is satisfied. The selected best subset then should be validated by prior knowledge/different tests through synthetic and/or real world data sets.

Feature selection in classification is being viewed as a most fundamental issue in machine learning. Major motivation is to select a feature subset, from which a learning rule is constructed, in sparse and interpretable rules, emphasizing few variables. Feature selection was studied widely in supervised learning scenarios in literature and its methods can be subdivided into filter methods and wrapper methods. The difference is that a wrapper method uses a classifier and a filter method does not. Wrapper approaches are clearly advantageous from a conceptual viewpoint as features selection is through optimizing a used classifier's discriminative power. Feature selection in unsupervised learning scenarios is bigger, due to class labels absence that searches for relevant information. Hence, wrapper selection strategies should be combined with clustering methods. A Gaussian mixture model is combined with a Bayesian feature selection principle. Combinatorial problems with wrapper approaches are offset by using a Bayesian marginalization mechanism.

Advantages of feature selection:

(i) It reduces feature space dimensionality, to reduce storage requirements and increase algorithm speed;

(ii) It removes redundant/irrelevant/noisy data.

(iii) Data analysis tasks immediate effects are speeding up learning algorithms running time.

(iv) Improving data quality.

(v) Increasing the resulting model's accuracy.

(vi) Feature set reduction, to save resources in next data collection round or when utilized;

(vii) Performance improvement resulting in predictive accuracy;

(viii) Data understanding to gain process knowledge that generated data or visualized data (Ladha, et al., 2011).

4.2 CLUSTERING

Data clustering is a popular data labeling technique where unlabeled data is issued, and similar samples put in one pile called a cluster with dissimilar samples being in other clusters. Generally, neither cluster description nor its quantification is given in advance unless domain knowledge exists, posing a challenge in data clustering.

Clustering is used in machine learning/data mining tasks including image segmentation, information retrieval, pattern recognition, pattern classification, and network analysis where it is either an exploratory task or preprocessing step. When the aim is to reveal hidden data patterns, clustering becomes an exploratory task by itself. Literature reveals many clustering methods which can be categorized into: partitioning methods, hierarchical methods, and density-based methods. Partitioning methods use distance-based metrics to cluster similarity based points (Alelyani et al 2013).

Clustering is also an unsupervised classification technique which when used on an objects set identifies inherent structures present in them through classification into subsets having some problem based contextual meaning. Objects with attributes characterizing them and represented as vectors in a multi-dimensional space are grouped into clusters. When clusters number, K, is known a priori, clustering can be a formulation as distribution of n objects in N dimensional space among K groups that objects in same cluster are similar in a sense than those in varied clusters which in turn needs minimization of extrinsic optimization criterion.

K-means algorithm, starting with k arbitrary cluster centers, partitions an objects set into k subsets and is a popular clustering technique due to ease of implementation and efficient with linear time complexity (Chen et al 2004). It has many drawbacks. K-means objective function is not convex and hence has many local minima. Thus, objective function minimization could be struck in local minima and at local maxima and saddle points (Selim, et al., 1984). K-means algorithm's outcome thus relies on cluster centers initial choice.

4.3 METHODOLOGY

4.3.1 Feature Selection Methods

The different types of Feature Selection are:

4.3.1.1 Filter method

Filter techniques assess feature relevance by looking at data's intrinsic properties alone. Usually, a feature relevance score is calculated and in most cases low-scoring features are removed. Later this features subset is presented as input to a classification algorithm. Filter techniques advantages include easy scalability to very high-dimensional datasets, computationally simple and fast and being independent of the classification algorithm. Hence, feature selection can be performed once for evaluation of different classifiers.

Filter method's common disadvantage is their ignoring classifier interaction (search in feature subset space is separated from search in hypothesis space), with most proposed techniques being univariate, meaning that each feature is considered separately, ignoring feature dependencies, which can result in worse classification performance when compared with other feature selection techniques. To overcome, the ignoring of feature dependencies, many multivariate filter techniques were introduced, all aimed at incorporating feature dependencies to some degree.

4.3.1.2 Wrapper Method

Wrapper methods are classifier-dependent. Selected feature subset's "goodness" is evaluated based on direct classification accuracy. Filter methods main advantage is low computation cost, due to the limited number of features used in classification. A small features number, even the "best," fail to guarantee high classification accuracy (Cover 1974; Elashoff et al 1967; Toussaint 1971). Wrapper methods lead to better performance as proved by many experiments (Kohavi and John 1997; Huang and Wang, 2006; Mao 2004; Yu and Cho 2006; Bi et al 2003; Sikora and Piramuthu 2007). Applications are limited by high computational complexity.

Support Vector Machines (SVM) was used as classifiers regularly in wrapper feature selection. Of the numerous wrapper algorithms used, Genetic Algorithm (GA), that solves optimization problems using evolution methods, specifically "survival of the fittest," proved promising thanks to its capability in solving global optimization issues(Raymer et al 2000; Yang and Li 2007; Yu and Cho 2003). Present GA-based wrapper methods were first developed for non-spatial datasets which have few such feature selection methods, speciallyhyper spectral data. And existing studies usually focused on feature subsets alone. SVM classifier's efficiency and accuracy are affected by the feature subset and also by kernel function, or kernel parameters if function was specified (Weston, et al., 2001). Also, feature subset/kernel parameters should both be optimized simultaneously to ensure optimal results (Huang and Wang 2006).

Wrapper algorithms have three main components (Guyon et al 2003):

(i)   Search algorithm,

(ii)   Fitness function, and

(iii) Inductive algorithm.

The wrapper approach conducts a search in possible parameters space. A search needs state space, initial state, termination condition, and search engine.

Algorithm 2: Ensemble Component (Yang):

Input: A feature subset **S**; Imbalanced training set **D**T and test set **D**t

Output: Fitness of **S**

1: $Fit = 0$;

2: // constrain the data dimension using the input feature subset:

3: $\mathbf{D}^S_T$= constrainDataDimension($\mathbf{D}_T$, **S**);

4: $E = \phi$

5: **for** $i = 1$ to L **do**

6: // Sampling to create a balanced dataset using training set:

7: $\mathbf{D_i}^{*S}$= hybridSampling($\mathbf{D}^S_T$);

8: // Train a base classifier using balanced dataset:

9: h_i= trainClassifier($\mathbf{D_i}^{*S}$);

10: // Add the base classifier to the ensemble:

11: $\mathbf{E} = \mathbf{E} \cup h_i$;

12: **end for**

13: $\mathbf{D}^S_t$= constrainDataDimension($\mathbf{D}_t$, **S**);

14: // Apply the ensemble of classifiers to the test set:

15: Fit = calculateAUC($\mathbf{E}, \mathbf{D}^S_t$);

16: **return** Fit;

4.3.1.3 Hybrid method

Embedded methods build prediction models that try to maximize the developed model's goodness of fit and minimize the model's input features number. Such methods are reliant on learning machine specifics used in prediction model. Embedded methods, including feature selection as part of training possess have some advantages like reaching a solution quicker by avoiding model retraining for each feature subset. It also makes better use of available data by not splitting it into training and validation subsets. Decision tree learning algorithms like CART inherently include an embedded feature selection method (Jashki et al 2009).

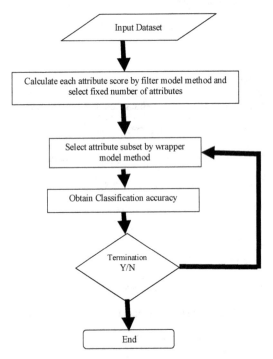

Figure 4.1 Hybrid filter and wrapper model feature selection method

Filter and wrapper methods are combined to select feature microarray genes, and use two different classification algorithms to evaluate the proposed method's performance. Figure 4.1 shows the hybrid filter and wrapper model feature selection method. The filter part uses Information Gain (IG) and Correlation-based Feature Selection (CFS) to evaluate each feature's ability to differentiate between various categories, the reasoning behind the two methods being that it can calculate each feature's importance with regard to class (Yang et al 2008).

4.3.2   Procedure of Feature Selection Evaluation

The filter model algorithm uses an independent criterion to evaluate the goodness of a feature/feature subset by exploiting training data's intrinsic characteristics without a mining algorithm. Independent criteria include distance measures, information measures, dependency measures, and consistency measures (Almuallim et al 1994; Ben-Bassat 1982; Hall 2000; Liu et al 1998).

Other names for distance measures are separabality, divergence, or discrimination measures. Information measures determine a feature's information gain. Dependency measures are also called correlation or similarity measures, and measures the ability to predict a variable's value from that of another. Consistency measures are characteristically differing from the above due to their reliance on class information and Min-Features bias (Almuallim et al 1994)use to select a features subset. Such measures try to locate minimum features number to separate classes consistently as a full set of features.

A wrapper model dependent criterion needs a predetermined feature selection mining algorithm and uses its performance applied on a selected subset to determine feature selection. As it locates features suited to predetermined mining algorithm it provides better performance, but is also computationally expensive and unsuited to other mining algorithms (Blum et al 1997). In clustering, feature selection through wrapper model evaluates a feature subset's goodness by cluster quality resulting from application of clustering algorithms on a selected subset.

4.3.3 Clustering for Feature Selection

Data clustering, an NP-complete problem of locating groups in heterogeneous data by minimizing some dissimilarity measure is a basic tool in data mining, machine learning and pattern classification solutions (Sung et al 2000). Clustering in N-dimensional Euclidean space, RN partitions a given set of n points into a number, say k, of groups (or, clusters) based on similarity (distance) metric in clustering procedure is Euclidean distance, derived from the Minkowski metric

$$d(x,y) = \left(\sum \right)^{1/r} \tag{4.1}$$

$$d(x,y) = \sqrt{\sum_{i=1}^{m} (x_i - y_j)^2} \tag{4.2}$$

A popular performance function to measure goodness of k clustering is the total within cluster variance or total mean-square quantization error (MSE) (Niknam et al 2008)

$$Per\, f(X,C) = \sum_{i=1}^{N} Min\{\|x_i - C_l\|^2 \mid l = 1,..K\} \tag{4.3}$$

The steps of the k-means algorithm are as follows (Krishna et al 1999):

Algorithm 3:

Step 1:   Choose K cluster centers

C1, C2, . . ., Ck randomly from n points $\{X1, X2, \ldots, Xn\}$.

Step 2:   Assign point Xi, $i = 1, 2, \ldots, n$ to cluster Cj,

$j \in \{ \ldots \} , \; \| \; _1 - \; _{j} \| < \| \; _1 - \; _{p} \| , \; \ldots, \; \neq p.$

Step 3:   Compute new cluster centers $C_1^*, C_2^*, \ldots, C_K^*$ as follows:

$$C_i^* = \frac{1}{n} \sum_{x_j \in C_i} x_j, \quad i = 1, 2, \ldots, K, \tag{4.4}$$

where n_i is the number of elements belonging to cluster C_i.

Step 4:   If termination criteria satisfied, stop otherwise continue from step 2.

Let $X = \{ \ldots \} \in \mathbb{R}^{\ldots \times n}$ denote the data set consisting of n samples over d-dimensional space, $S_{ij} (0 \le _y \le \infty)$ denote the similarity between the points x_i and x_j, and the similarity matrix $S = \begin{bmatrix} \quad \end{bmatrix}_{\ldots \times n}$ is assumed to be symmetric. An intuitive clustering objective is to seek the partition such that the summation of similarities between points in the same cluster is maximized, while that in different cluster is minimized. Such a criterion can be realized to maximize the following cost function:

$$\Box(\Box) = \sum_{l=}^{k} \left[\sum_\Box \Box \qquad \sum_\Box \right] \tag{4.5}$$

where C is a possible partition, k is the number of clusters which is assumed known, C_l is the set of points contained in the l-th cluster $(1 \le \le k)$, and the number of points in the l-th cluster is denoted by $|Cl|(|Cl|\le n)$(Zeng et al 2008).

4.3.4   Particle Swarm Optimization

Particle Swarm Optimization (PSO) is a recent heuristic search method inspired by the swarming/collaborative behavior of biological populations. PSO is similar to Genetic Algorithm (GA) in that both evolutionary heuristics are population-based search methods. A randomly generated set of solutions (initial swarm) in a PSO propagates in design space towards optimal solution over much iteration dependent on huge information about design space assimilated and shared by all swarm members. PSO is inspired by the combined abilities of bird flocks, fish schools animal herds to adapt to local environments, locate rich food sources and avoid predators through implementation of an "information sharing" approach, which thereby develops an evolutionary advantage.

The PSO algorithm includes three steps; generating particles' positions and velocities, velocity update, and position update. A particle refers to a design space point which changes its position from one move (iteration) to another based on velocity updates. First, positions, x_i^k, and velocities, v_i^k, of initial particles swarm are randomly generated using design variable values upper and lower bounds,x_{min} and x_{max} , as expressed in Equations 1 and 2. Positions/velocities are given in a vector format with superscript and subscript denoting the i^{th}particle at time k. In Equations 1 and 2, *rand* is a uniformly distributed random variable that takes any value between 0 and 1. Initialization ensures swarm particles to be randomly distributed across design space (Hassan et al 2005).

$$x_0^i = _{\text{min}} + (_{\text{max}} - x_{\text{min}})$$
$$v_0^i = \frac{x_{\text{min}} + (_{\text{max}} - x_{\text{min}})}{\Box t} = \frac{position}{time} \qquad (4.6)$$

In common PSO implementations particles move through search space combining an attraction to a best solution found individually and an attraction to a best solution found by any particle in their *neighborhood*. A neighborhood in PSO is defined for an individual particle as particles subset which can communicate with it. The first PSO used a Euclidian neighborhood for particle communication, measuring actual distance between particles to determine communication between those close enough for this task. This imitated bird flock behavior, the same as biological models, where individual birds can communicate with others in the vicinity (Reynolds 1987; Heppner et al 1990). Euclidian neighborhood model was given up favoring less computationally intensive models as research shifted from biological modeling to mathematical optimization.

Particle Representation

In the context of clustering, a single particle represents cluster centroid vectors. That is, each particle X_{ij}, is constructed as follows:

$$X_{ij} = (m_{i1}, m_{i2}, \ldots, m_{im})$$

where m_{ij} refers to the j-th cluster centroid vector of the i-th particle in cluster C_{ij}. Hence, a swarm represents many candidates clustering for current data vectors.

Initial Population

One swarm particle represents a possible clustering solution. So, a swarm represents many candidate data set clustering solutions. Initially, each particle chooses randomly k different data set from a collection as initial cluster centroid vectors and data sets are assigned to clusters based on K-Means iteration.

Local search

After locating solutions of N particles, a local search further improves solutions fitness. Local search generates better solutions, when heuristic information is not discovered easily. Local search is applicable on all generated solutions or on a few percent N.

Personal best & Global best positions of particle

A particle's personal best position is calculated as follows

$$P_{id}(t+) = \begin{cases} + \geq f(P_{id}(t)) \\ X_{id}(t+) + < f(P_{id}(t)) \end{cases} \tag{4.7}$$

The particle to be attracted to the best swarm particle is global best position of every particle. At the beginning, initial particle position is considered as *personal best* and *global best is* identified with a minimum fitness function value.

In PSO algorithms, the above operations are iterated in main loop till a specific iterations number is completed or all particles start generating similar results. This is called stagnation behavior, as after a point, the algorithm generates alternative solutions (Premalatha et al 2008).

102

A pseudo code for algorithm (Elshamy et al 2007):

Algorithm 4:

> **begin**
>
> Initialize particles and clubs
>
> **while**(termination condition = false)
>
> **do**
>
> evaluate particles fitness: $f(x)$
>
> update P
>
> **for**(i = 1 to number of particles)
>
> gi = best of neighborsi
>
> **for**d= 1 to number of dimensions
>
> vid = $\times \quad {}^{,,}\times {}^{,,} + {}^{,}\ {}^{,}\times \quad {}^{,\gamma}\times({}^{,,} \quad {}^{,,}) + {}^{,}\ {}^{\gamma}\times \quad {}^{,\gamma}\times({}^{,,} -x\text{id})$
>
> xid = ,, +vid
>
> **next**d
>
> **next**i
>
> update neighbors
>
> **for**j= 1 to number of particles
>
> **if**(xj is best of neighborsj) and ($|$membershipj$|$ >min_membership)
>
> leave random club
>
> **end if**
>
> **if**(xj is worst of neighborsj) and ($|$membershipj$|$ <max_membership)
>
> join random club
>
> **end if**

if($|$membershipj$|$ $\neq$ default_membership) and (remainder(iteration/rr) = 0)

updatemembershipj

end if

next j

end do

iteration = iteration + 1

evaluate termination condition

end while

4.3.5 Genetic Algorithm For Clustering

Genetic algorithms (GAs) (Goldberg et al 1989; Davis et al 1991; Michalewicz et al 1992; Filho et al 1994) are randomized search/optimization techniques guided by evolution and natural genetics principles, with a huge amount of implicit parallelism. Search in complex, large and multimodal landscapes are performed by GAs providing near-optimal solutions for an optimization problem's objective/ fitness function. Parameters of search space are encoded in strings (called *chromosomes*) in G As. A collection of strings is a *population*. A random population is initially created representing various search space points. An *objective* and *fitness* functions are associated with each string representing the string's *goodness* degree. Based on the survival of the fittest principle, a few more strings are selected with each being assigned many copies that go to a mating pool. Biologically inspired operators like *cross over* and *mutation* are applied on strings yielding a new strings generation. The selection process including crossover and mutation continues for specific generations or till a termination condition is reached(Pal et al 1994; Whitley et al 1990; Belew et al 1991; Forrest et al 1993; Eshelman et al 1995).

GAs work with an *individuals population* representing feasible solutions as abstract representations. Each individual is assigned a *fitness* that measures the goodness of the solution it represents. The better, a solution, the higher is its fitness value. The population evolves to better solutions and evolution starts from a population of completely random individuals iterating in generations. An individual's fitness is evaluated in each generation. Individuals are selected stochastically from a current population (fitness based), and modified through operators *mutation* and *crossover* to create a new population (Kudova 2007).

Selection method

A selection method defines construction of a new generation of S individuals from the current one. Selection includes the following three steps:

(i)   determining SB survivors

(ii) selecting a crossing set of SC individuals

(iii) selecting pairs for crossover from crossing set

Crossover operations

A crossover operation produces a new solution ωn from two parent solutions ωa and ωb.

Mutations

A randomly chosen data set replaces each cluster centroid with probability ψ, the operation being performed after crossover.

Noise

Noise is added to centroids after mutation by adding a random vector to each centroid. The component values of this vector are in $(-v, v)$ range.

Fine-tuning by the k-means algorithm

G iterations of k-means algorithm are applied to fine-tune new solutions which compensates the fact that crossover, mutation and noise operations are unlikely to produce better solutions (Kivijärvi, et al., 2003).

Genetic Algorithm:

Algorithm 5:

1. Create randomly an initial population P0 of M individual.

2. $i \leftarrow 0$

3. Evaluate fitness for individuals from Pi.

4. If the stop criterion is satisfied, stop and return the best individual.

5. Pi+1 $\leftarrow$ empty set

6. I1 $\leftarrow$ selection(Pi); I2 $\leftarrow$ selection(Pi)

7. With probability pc: (I1, I2) $\leftarrow$ crossover(I1, I2)

8. With probability pm: Ik $\leftarrow$ mutate(Ik), k = 1, 2

9. Insert I1, I2 into Pi+1.

10. If Pi+1 has less then M individuals goto 6.

11. $i \leftarrow i + 1$ Goto 3.

GA clustering is a GA based clustering technique whose searching capability is exploited to search for appropriate cluster centers in feature space so that resulting clusters similarity metrics is optimized. Chromosomes, represented as real number strings, encode centers of fixed clusters number. GA-clustering algorithm's superiority over K-means algorithm is demonstrated through four artificial and three real-life data sets.

The feature selection filter method for clustering consists of looking for a SA sub set to minimize $fit(SA, SA_*)$ function. This search though exhaustive implies a high computational cost which is reduced through use of GA performing only a partial space exploration composed by SA subsets.

GA used is defined as follows:

(i) A chromosome codes (corresponds to) a SA subset;

(ii) Each chromosome gene codes a SA attribute(so, there are l genes);

(iii) Each chromosome gene has a binary value: gene value is 1 (resp. 0) if associated attribute is present (resp. absent) in SA subset coded by the chromosome.

The FS algorithm is given next; it should be noted that:

(i) It requires only 1dataset scan (due to $Aq1$ and $Aq2$ properties);

(ii) It stores some contingency tables (due to $Aq1\&Aq2$) which only correspond to a limited memory(typically fits into computer main memory);

(iii) Its complexity is small (it is quadratic based on number of dataset attributes and totally independent from objects number once needed contingency tables are built) (due to $Aq1$ and $Aq2$ properties) ;

(iv) It deals either with numerical, categorical or mixed categorical and numerical data.

Algorithm: *Filter Feature Selection for Clustering*

(i) In a dataset scan derive the $\frac{l(l-1)}{2}$ contingency tables necessary to compute previously presented adequacy indices.

(ii) Run GA using fitness function $fit(SA; SA*)$.

(iii) Select best subspace located by GA.

4.3.6   Proposed Methodology

PSO's drawback is that the swarm may converge prematurely. The principle on which this problem is based is that for global best PSO, particles converge on a single point on the line between global best and personal best positions and this point is not guaranteed for local optimum (Bergh and Engelbrecht 2004). Another reason is the information flow rate between particles leading to the creation of similar particles with a diversity loss increasing the possibility of a local optima trap.

Another drawback is that stochastic approaches provide problem-dependent performance. This dependency is due to each algorithm's parameter settings. A stochastic search algorithm's differing parameter settings leads to high performance variances. Usually no single parameter setting is applicable for all problems. Increasing inertia weight (w) increases particles speed resulting in more exploration (global search) and less exploitation (local search). On the other hand, reduction of inertia weight decreases particles speed leading to more exploitation/less exploration. So finding the parameter's best value is not easy and it can differ from one problem to another. Hence, it can be concluded that PSO performance is problem-dependent which can be addressed through hybrid mechanisms. It combines various approaches and benefits from each approach's advantages.

Hybrid algorithms with GA are proposed to overcome PSO limitations, the basis behind being that a hybrid approach will have PSO's merits with those of GA. PSO's advantage over GA is its algorithmic simplicity with another difference being its convergence controlling ability. Crossover and mutation rates affect GA convergence subtly, but cannot be analogous to control achieved through inertia weight manipulation. Inertia weight decrease increases swarm convergence. PSO's problem is premature convergence (Bergh and Engelbrecht 2004) to a stable point, not necessarily maximum. Global best particles position update is changed to prevent this. Position update is undertaken through GA's hybrid mechanism. The idea behind GA is based on its genetic operators, crossover and mutation. Information is swapped between two particles through crossover application which can fly to a new search area. The purpose of mutation application to PSO is to increase population diversity and to ensure that PSO avoids local maxima.

Cooperative search is a parallel algorithm, where several search algorithms run in parallel to solve optimization issues. As search algorithms differ, cooperative search technique is considered a hybrid algorithm. This work proposes to implement a Hybrid Evolutionary Algorithm using GA and PSO. The latter both work in the proposed system with same population. Initially, Ps individuals forming the population are generated randomly and are considered GA chromosomes or PSO particles. New next generation individuals are created by enhancement, crossover, and mutation operations after initialization. Figure 4.2 reveals the architecture of the proposed hybrid algorithm.

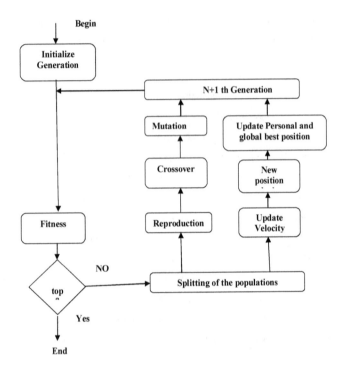

Figure 4.2 Flowchart of the proposed Hybrid Algorithm incorporating GA and PSO

4.4 EXPERIMENTAL SETUP AND RESULTS

Reuters and MovieLens datasets are used to evaluate the proposed methods. Experiments are conducted as stated in the previous chapter, with the proposed feature selection being included. Precision values for various techniques for MovieLens and Reuters datasets are evaluated. Techniques used include tdf.idf, Language modelling with query likelihood, proposed concept expansion and proposed DNLM with the proposed feature selection.

Results for precision and F measure for MovieLens dataset are tabulated in Table 4.1 and Table 4.2 respectively. Figure 4.3 and 4.4 reveal the same.

Table 4.1 Precision values for various techniques for MovieLens dataset

Recall	TDF-IDF	Concept expansion	Language modelling using Query likelihood	Proposed DNLM
0.01	0.70599168	0.756156806	0.7361777	0.8260681
0.1	0.6465462	0.713912832	0.6947029	0.77992079
0.2	0.6271396	0.6455375	0.65530184	0.7052309
0.3	0.6250968	0.63830748	0.62834322	0.69731398
0.4	0.57433322	0.61248598	0.59308964	0.66908391
0.5	0.5525774	0.59079592	0.57857346	0.64543732
0.6	0.5025288	0.58666448	0.56198354	0.64095801
0.7	0.47004828	0.55154724	0.54020927	0.60251928
0.8	0.4300094	0.51746286	0.5080663	0.56533059
0.9	0.41887614	0.47924704	0.44792784	0.52355842
1	0.23573912	0.403951546	0.37534694	0.3343857

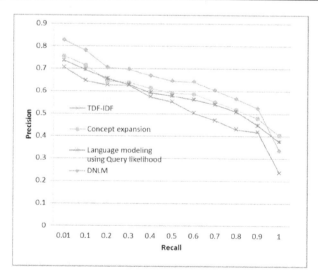

Figure 4.3 Precision values for various techniques for MovieLens dataset

From the figure 4.3 it is seen that precision values for DNLM with the proposed feature selection is higher than the precision values for all the other techniques. The precision values for DNLM with the proposed feature selection is higher than the precision values for tdf.idf by 17% when recall is 0.01 and 25% when recall is 0.9. DNLM with the proposed feature selection performs better than concept expansion by 9.2% when recall is 0.01 and 0.9. Similarly for Language modelling using query likelihood, DNLM with the proposed feature selection performs better by 12.2 % when recall is 0.01 and 16.8% when recall is 0.09.

Table 4.2 Average F measure values for various techniques for MovieLens dataset

	TDF-IDF	Concept expansion	Language modelling using Query likelihood	Proposed DNLM
F measure	0.513272862	0.542049221	0.535195392	0.560209909

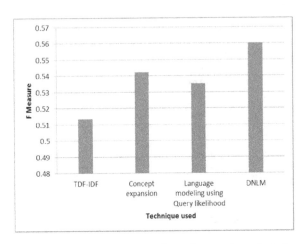

Figure 4.4 Average F measure values for various techniques for MovieLens dataset

From the Figure 4.4 it is seen that average f measure values for DNLM with the proposed feature selection is higher than the average f measure values for all the other techniques. The average f measure values for DNLM with the proposed feature selection is higher than the average f measure values for tdf.idf by 9.1%, concept expansion by 3.3% and Language modelling using query likelihood by 4.6 %.

The experimental results for Reuters-21758 dataset for precision and F measure are tabulated in Table 4.3 and Table 4.4 respectively. Figure 4.5 and 4.6 show the same.

Table 4.3   Precision values for various techniques for Reuters-21758 dataset

Recall	TDF-IDF	Concept expansion	Language modelling using Query likelihood	Proposed DNLM
0.01	0.781	0.8365	0.8144	0.9138
0.1	0.7152	0.7897	0.7685	0.8628
0.2	0.6937	0.7141	0.7249	0.7801
0.3	0.6915	0.7061	0.6951	0.7714
0.4	0.6353	0.6775	0.6561	0.7401
0.5	0.6113	0.6535	0.64	0.714
0.6	0.5559	0.649	0.6217	0.709
0.7	0.52	0.6101	0.5976	0.6665
0.8	0.4757	0.5724	0.562	0.6254
0.9	0.4634	0.5301	0.4955	0.5792
1	0.2608	0.4469	0.4152	0.3699

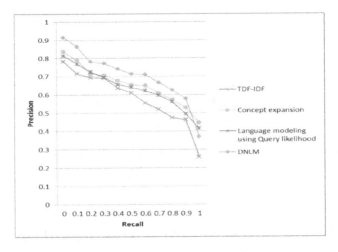

Figure 4.5   Precision values for various techniques for Reuters-21758 dataset

The Figure 4.5 shows the relationship between precision and recall for Reuters-21758 dataset and it is seen that precision values for DNLM with the proposed feature selection are higher when compared with the precision values for all the other techniques. The precision values for DNLM with the proposed feature selection is higher than the precision values for tdf.idf by 17% when recall is 0.01and 25% when recall is 0.9. DNLM with the proposed feature selection performs better than concept expansion by 9.2% when recall is 0.01and 0.9. Similarly for Language modelling using query likelihood, DNLM with the proposed feature selection performs better by 12.2 % when recall is 0.01 and 11.2% when recall is 0.09.

Table 4.4 Average F measure values for various techniques for Reuters-21758 dataset

	TDF-IDF	Concept expansion	Language modelling using Query likelihood	DNLM
F measure	0.537962667	0.566447788	0.559682972	0.584347274

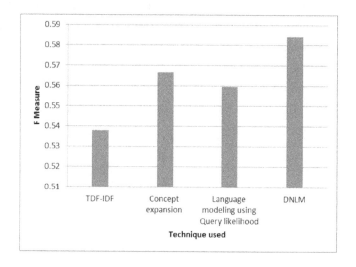

Figure 4.6 Average F measure values for various techniques for Reuters-21758 dataset

From the above pictorial representation it is seen that the proposed methodology produces higher average f measure than the existing tf.idf method, concept expansion and Language modelling using Query likelihood. The average f measure values for DNLM with the proposed feature selection is higher than the average f measure values for tdf.idf by 8.6%, concept expansion by 3.1 %, and Language modelling using query likelihood by 4.4%.

4.5   CONCLUSION

This work proposes a feature selection method based on hybrid optimization to solve nonlinear partitioned clustering problem. PSO and GA are the basis for the hybrid algorithm. A hybrid approach is expected to have the merits of both PSO and GA. PSO's advantage over GA is its algorithmic simplicity with another difference between them being convergence control ability. Experiments reveals that the proposed feature with proposed DNLM method ensures better recall when compared with traditional tdf.idf and Language modelling using Query likelihood.

CHAPTER 5

CONCEPT BASED QUERY EXPANSION

5.1   INTRODUCTION

Language Modelling (LM) is used in many IR studies producing good experimental results (comparable to best IR systems), and also a solid theoretical setting. Classical LM approaches are not dependent between indexing units, which are unigrams or bigrams. A word can be related to other words. An example is synonymy relationship as such intra-term relationships should be integrated into LM.

Present information retrieval systems like web search engines consist of a standard interface of a single input box which accepts keywords. User submitted key words are matched against a collection index to locate documents with those keywords, sorted out by various methods. When a user query has multiple topic-specific keywords accurately describing needed information, the system will return good matches; but as user queries are short with inherently ambiguous natural language, this retrieval model is prone to errors/omissions.

A critical language issue for effective retrieval is term mismatch problem: indexers and users do not use similar words usually. This is a vocabulary problem (Furnas et al 1987), compounded by synonymy and polysemy. Synonymy with word inflections (plural forms), fail to retrieve relevant documents, with a recall decrease (the system's ability to retrieve relevant documents). Polysemy which are different words with same/similar meanings can lead to erroneous or irrelevant document retrieval, thereby implying a precision decrease (system's ability to retrieve relevant documents).To offset this issue many approaches were proposed including relevance feedback, search results clustering ,interactive query refinement and word sense disambiguation. A successful technique is expanding original query with other words which capture best user intent or produce a useful query, i.e., a query that will retrieve relevant documents. Automatic query expansion (AQE) has an IR history suggested by Maron and Kuhns (1960) which investigated many seminal techniques that were later improved and extended in ways like vector feedback (Rocchio 1971; Ide 1971), term-term clustering (Lesk 1969; Harper and Rijsbergen 1978), and comparative analysis of term distributions (Doszkocs 1978; Porter 1982). Many small scale experiments resulted in inconclusive results about retrieval effectiveness of techniques, with gain in recall compensated by corresponding precision loss.

Query expansion methods were long studied - with debatable success on many occasions. This study presents a probabilistic query expansion model based on similarity thesaurus constructed automatically. The latter reflects domain knowledge about specific collections from which it is constructed. Two important issues with query expansion are addressed here: selection and weighting of additional search terms. Compared to earlier methods, queries are expanded by addition of terms similar to query concept, instead of selecting terms similar to query terms.

5.2   QUERY EXPANSION

As data volume dramatically increased while searcher supplied query terms remained very low, it led to a revamp of research on Query Expansion. Web search is a case in point. According to Hitwise (http://www.hitwise.com/), average query length was of 2.30 words in 2009, same as that reported ten years earlier in (Lau and Horvitz 1999). While there was a slight increase in long queries numbers (of five or more words), most prevalent queries were still those of one, two, or three words. Thus, the vocabulary problem is still more serious as query terms paucity reduces chances of handling synonymy while data heterogeneity and size make polysemy effects more severe.

The need/scope of Automatic Query Expansion (AQE) increased. Recently, many AQE techniques were presented with varied approaches leveraging many data sources and using sophisticated methods to find query term correlated new features. Now, there are firm theoretical foundations and better understanding of AQE utility and limitations; e.g., critical parameters affecting method performance, what type of queries AQE is useful for, etc. Simultaneously, basic techniques are increasingly used along with other mechanisms to increase effectiveness, including method combination, active selection of information sources, and method application's discriminative policies. These scientific advances were corroborated by positive experimental findings in laboratory settings. In fact, AQE regained popularity due to evaluation results from Text REtrieval Conference series (TREC,http://trec.nist.gov/), where most participants who used this technique reported noticeable retrieval performance improvement.

AQE is now a promising technique to improve document ranking retrieval effectiveness and that it is being adopted in commercial applications, mainly in desktop and intranet searches. For instance, Google Enterprise, My SQL and Lucene provide users with AQE facility capable of being turned on/off. It is yet to be regularly used in major operational web IR systems like search engines.

There are many reasons for AQE's limited uptake in web search. First, fast response times needed by web search applications prevent use of computationally expensive AQE techniques. Second, current AQE techniques though optimized to perform well on average, are unstable and cause degradation of search service in some queries. Also AQE emphasis on improving recall (as opposed to guaranteeing high precision) is less important, as there are relevant documents with many users looking only at first and last page for results. Third, AQE acceptance is an issue, due to limited usability and IR system transparency when implementing AQE: the user may be confused when system retrieves documents without original query terms. But such features are less important in many IR applications (search by experts in specialized domains), where a straightforward AQE application has no major contraindications.

5.2.1   Applications of AQE

The different applications of AQE are

5.2.1.1   Question answering

Question answering (QA) goal is providing concise responses (instead of full documents) to some natural language questions like "What are the different forms of worship in India?" Similar to document ranking, QA faces a fundamental mismatch problem between question and answer vocabularies.

5.2.1.2   Multimedia information retrieval

With digital media and libraries increasing, multimedia documents (e.g., speech, image, and video) search is widely used. Generally, multimedia IR systems use text-based search over media metadata like annotations, captions, and surrounding html/xml descriptions. When metadata is absent, IR relies on some multimedia form of content analysis, combined with AQE techniques.

5.2.1.3   Information filtering

Information filtering (IF) monitors a stream of documents, selecting those relevant to a user. Documents arrive continuously and user's information need evolves over time. Examples of filtering application domains are blogs, e-mail, e-commerce, and electronic news.

5.2.1.4   Cross-language information retrieval

Cross-Language Information Retrieval (CLIR) retrieves documents written in a language other than the user's query language.

5.2.1.5   Other applications of AQE

Other AQE applications include

(i)   Text categorization ((Zelikovitz and Hirsh 2000), (Hidalgo et al 2005)),

(ii)   Search of hidden web content not indexed by standard search engines (Graupmann et al 2005),

(iii)   Mobile devices query completion (Kamvar and Baluja 2007),

(iv)   e-commerce (Chen, et al., 2004),

(v)   Mobile search(Church and Smyth 2007),

(vi)   Training corpora acquisition (Huang, et al., 2005; Perugini and Ramakrishnan 2006),

(vii)   Expert finding (Macdonald and Ounis 2007),

(viii) Federated search (Shokouhi et al 2009),

(ix) Paid search advertising (Wang et al 2009; Broder et al 2009), and

(x) Slot-based document retrieval (Suryanto et al 2007)

5.2.2 AQE Process

AQE is broken into 4 steps as shown in Figure 5.1: data source preprocessing; candidate expansion features generation and ranking; expansion features selection and query reformulation.

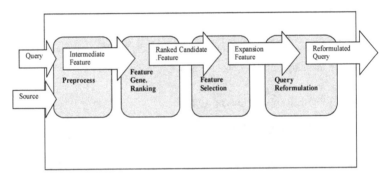

Figure 5.1 Main steps of automatic query expansion

Data source preprocessing transforms raw data source used to expand user query into a format more effectively processed by subsequent steps. It consists of a phase of intermediate features extraction, followed by appropriate data structures construction for easy access to and their manipulation. Data source preprocessing is independent of a particular user query to be expanded but specific to data source type and expansion method under consideration. Many query expansion techniques are based on information contained in top-ranked items retrieved in response to document collection's original user query. To compute initial retrieval run, the collection should be indexed and then run query against it.

In second AQE stage, system generates and ranks candidate expansion features. The reason for its importance is that query expansion methods choose only a limited proportion of candidate expansion features to add to query.

Original query is the input to this stage and the transformed data source; output is an expansion features set, usually with associated scores. Original query is preprocessed to remove common words and/or extract important terms for expansion (importance being approximated e.g., by their inverse document frequency).

After candidate features ranking, top elements are chosen for query expansion. Selection is on individual basis, without considering mutual dependencies between expansion features. This is a simple assumption though there are experimental results that suggest that independence assumption is justified (Lin and Murray 2005).Usually limited features are selected for expansion, partly as resulting query can be processed rapidly and partly because retrieval effectiveness of a small set of good terms is not less successful than combining candidate expansion terms, due to noise reduction; (Salton and Buckley 1990; Harman 1992).

The last AQE step is query reformulation; how to describe expanded query to be submitted to the IR system, usually amounting to assigning a weight to each feature describing expanded query – termed query reweighting. One of the commonly used query reweighting technique is modeled after Rocchio's formula for relevance feedback (Rocchio 1971) and later improvements (Salton and Buckley1990), adapted to an AQE setting.

123

5.2.3   Methods of AQE

Automatic query expansion/modification based on term data co-occurrence was studied for nearly thirty years. Various methods in literature are classified in the following four groups:

(i)   *Simple co-occurrence data use*: Similarities between terms are calculated based on association hypothesis and used to classify terms through a similarity threshold value (Lesk 1969;Minkar et al 1972). Thus, an index terms set is subdivided into similar terms classes. A query is expanded by adding all classe's terms containing query terms. The idea of term classification into classes and treating members of same class as equivalent was too naive an approach to be good (Sparck-Jones 1991).

(ii)   *Document classification use*: Documents are classified through a document classification algorithm. Infrequent terms in a document class are taken to be similar and clustered in same term class (thesaurus class) (Crouch 1990). Indexing of documents and queries is enhanced by replacing a term by a thesaurus class or adding a thesaurus class to index data. Retrieval effectiveness depends on parameters which are hard to determine (Crouch and Yong 1992). Further, commercial databases have millions of documents all of which are highly dynamic. Document number is larger than terms number in the database. Hence, document classification is more expensive and should be undertaken more often than simple term classification.

(iii)   *Syntactic context use*: Term relations are generated based on linguistic knowledge and co-occurrence statistics (Grefenstette

1992;Ruge 1992) using grammar and a dictionary to extract a list of terms for each term t. This contains all terms that modify t. Similarities between terms are calculated using modifiers from the list. Then a query is expanded by adding terms similar to any query term producing only slightly better results than using original queries (Grefenstette 1992).

(iv) *Relevance information use*: Relevance information constructs a global information structure, a pseudo thesaurus (Saltonand Buckley 1980) or a minimum spanning tree (Smeaton and Rijsbergen1983). A query is expanded by this global information structure. This method's retrieval effectiveness depends on user relevance information. Moreover, experiments failed to yield consistent improvement in performance. But, direct use of relevance information by extracting terms from relevant documents was effective in interactive information retrieval (Harman 1992; Sal1990). This approach does not help queries without relevance information. Semi-automatic query expansion was also studied (Hancock-Beaulieu 1992). In contrast to fully automated methods, user is involved in selecting additional search terms in a semi-automatic expansion process. A list of candidate terms is computed by one of the above methods and presented to the user who finally decides. Semi-automatic query expansion experiments did not result in major improvement in retrieval effectiveness (Ekmekcioglu et al 1992).

Among many approaches, automatic query expansion through using plain co-occurrence data is the simplest. Compared to present approaches, a similarity thesaurus (Schäuble and Knaus 1992) is the basis of query expansion. First the similarity thesaurus construction is shown and then a query expansion model is presented to overcome drawbacks in using plain co-occurrence data.

5.3   DOCUMENT RANKING WITH AQE

IR systems and search engines mostly rely on computing terms importance in the query and in documents to determine answers. Similarity sim(q, d) between query q and document d can be expressed as

$$sim(q,d) = \sum_{t \in q \cap d} w_{t,q}.w_{t,d} \qquad (5.1)$$

where $w_{t,q}$ is weight of term t in query q and w_{td} is weight of term in document d, respectively, according to system's weighting function. A term's weight is proportional to term frequency and inversely proportional to frequency and documents length having the term. This formulation accounts for several ranking models that are directly or indirectly traced it, including probabilistic relevance model (Robertson, et al., 1998), vector space model (Salton and McGill 1983), statistical language modelling (Zhaiand Lafferty, 2001), and deviation from randomness (Amati et al 2001).

The formula of ranking scheme is modified to accommodate query expansion, abstracting from specific underlying weighting model. The AQE input consists of original query q and a data source which computes and weights expansion terms. AQE output is a query q' formed by an expanded terms set with associated weights w'. New weighted query terms compute similarity between query q' and document d:

$$sim(q',d) = \sum_{t \in q' \cap d} w'_{t,q'}.w_{t,d} \qquad (5.2)$$

Typical data sources to generate new terms is a collection being searched itself and simplest way to weight query expansion terms is by using weighting function of the ranking system. If complex features than single terms are used for query expansion (phrases), underlying ranking must handle such features.

5.4   PROPOSED CONCEPT BASED QUERY EXPANSION

A similarity thesaurus (Schäuble and Knaus 1992) is a matrix consisting of term-term similarities. Compared to a co-occurrence matrix, similarity thesaurus is based on how collection terms are "indexed" by documents. It is shown that a similarity thesaurus is built automatically using arbitrary retrieval with documents roles and terms interchanged. Terms play role of retrievable items and documents constitute their "indexing features."

With this, a term t_i is represented by a vector in document vector space (DVS) defined by all documents of the collection. The d_{ik}'s signify feature weights of the indexing features of documented with respect to the term t_i and n being the collection's features (documents) number. The normalized tf.idf weighting scheme (Salton and Buckley 1988) is adopted and defines feature weights d_{ik} by feature frequency (ff), inverse item frequency (iif), and maximum feature frequency (maxff) as follows.

$$d_{ik} = \frac{(0.5+0.5\frac{ff(d_k,t_i)}{\max ff(t_i)}).iif(d_k)}{\sqrt{\sum_{j=1}^{n}((0.5+0.5\frac{ff(d_j,t_i)}{\max ff(t_i)}).iif(d_j))^2}} \tag{5.3}$$

where $ff(d_k,t_i)$ is the within-item frequency of feature d_k in term t_i .

$iif(dk) = \log(m/|dk|)$ is the inverse item frequency of featured$_k$

m is the number of items in the collection and $|dk|$ is number of different items indexed by feature d_k.

$|dk|$ is the number of terms appearing in document dk.maxff(t_i) is maximum within-item frequency of features in item t_i.

Feature frequency ff(d_k, t_i) specifies the occurrences number of d_k in t_i. It is analogous to term frequency tf(t_i, d_k) when documents are indexed by terms. Definition of inverse item frequency reveals that a short document has an important role than a longer one. When two terms co-occur in a long document, the probability that two terms are similar is lesser than if they co-occurred in a short document. It is then derived that

$$|\vec{t_i}| = \sqrt{\sum_{k=1}^{n} d_{ik}^2} = 1 \tag{5.4}$$

Thus, t_i is a unit vector representing term in document vector space DVS. These definitions define similarity between two terms t_i and t_j through using a similarity measure like a simple scalar vector product:

$$SIM(t_i, t_j) = \vec{t_i}.\vec{t_j} = \sum_{k=1}^{n} d_{ik}.d_{jk} \tag{5.5}$$

Similarity thesaurus is built through determining similarities of all term pairs (t_i, t_j), resulting in a symmetric matrix whose values are in the following range:

$$0 \leq \cdots \left({}_{\left(\begin{smallmatrix} \\ i' \end{smallmatrix} \right)} \right) \leq 1$$

A query q is represented by a vector q = $(q1, q2, ..., qm)^T$ in term vector space (TVS) defined by all collection terms. Here, the q_i's are weights of the search terms t_i contained in query q; m is total number of collection terms.

Probability that term t is similar to query concept q is $P(S|q,t)$. Bayes' theorem is applied to estimate probability:

$$P(S|q,t) = P(S|t) \cdot \frac{P(q|S,t)}{P(q|t)} = \frac{P(S|t)}{P(q|t)} \cdot P(q|S,t) \quad (5.6)$$

It is assumed that terms distribution in all queries which has a similar term is independent:

$$
\begin{aligned}
P(S|q,t) &= \frac{P(S|t)}{P(q|t)} \cdot \prod_{i=1}^{m} P(q_i|S,t) \\
&= \frac{P(S|t)}{P(q|t)} \cdot \prod_{i=1}^{m} \frac{P(S|q_i,t)}{P(S|t)} \cdot P(q_i|t) \\
&= \frac{1}{P(q|t).P(S|t)^{m-1}} \cdot \prod_{i=1}^{m} P(S|q_i,t).P(q_i|t)
\end{aligned}
\quad (5.7)
$$

Another assumption is that similarity between a term and query concept depends on terms in the query and no other terms. Hence,

$$P(S|q,t) = \frac{1}{P(q|t).P(S|t)^{m-1}} \cdot \prod_{t_i \in q} P(S|t_i,t).P(t_i|t) \quad (5.8)$$

$P(S|t_i,t)$ is the probability that query term t_i is similar to term t. $P(t_i|t)$ is probability that query term ti represents query q. $P(q|t)$ is the probability that query q will be submitted to IR system. $P(S|t)$ is probability that term t is similar to an arbitrary query.

The probability of a term being similar to a query is based on factors which follow:

(i)   Similarities between term and all query terms;

(ii)   Weights of query terms.

The objective of this query expansion scheme is to locate suitable additional query terms having properties similar to the entire query rather than individual query terms. It was shown that such terms are found when overall similarity scheme is considered. As similarity thesaurus expresses similarity between collection terms in DVS (defined by collection documents), vector q is mapped from TVS (defined by collection terms) into vector in space DVS. Thus, overall similarity between a term and query is estimated. Every query term t_i is defined by unit vector t_i which in turn is defined by a documents number. q_i is weight of term t_i in query. The concept expressed by term t_i in query has importance of $q_i .t_i$ for query. It is assumed that concept expressed by the whole query depends on query terms alone. Hence, vector q_c representing query concept in DVS space is virtual term vector:

$$\vec{q}_c = \sum_{t_i \in q} q_i \vec{t}_i \tag{5.9}$$

Similarity between a term and query q is denoted by Simqt(q,t). Scalar vector product is used as similarity measure:

$$Sim\ qt(q,t) = \vec{q}_c^{\,T} \vec{t} = (\overline{\sum_{t_i \in q} q_i \vec{t}_i})^{t} \vec{t}$$
$$= \sum_{t_i \in q} q_i . (\vec{t}_i^{\,T} \vec{t}) \tag{5.10}$$

where $\left(t_i^{\,T}.t \right)$ is the similarity between two terms.

5.5 EXPERIMENTAL SETUP AND RESULTS

The Reuters dataset and MovieLens dataset is used for evaluating the proposed methods. The experiments are conducted as detailed in the previous chapter, with the inclusion of proposed concept query expansion method. Precision values for various techniques for MovieLens dataset and Reuters dataset is evaluated. The techniques used were tdf.idf, Language modelling using query likelihood, proposed concept expansion and proposed DNLM with the proposed feature selection method. The experimental results for MovieLens dataset for precision and F measure are tabulated in Table 5.1 and Table 5.2 respectively. Figure 5.2 and 5.3 show the same.

Table 5.1 Precision values for various techniques for MovieLens dataset

Recall	TDF-IDF	Concept expansion	Language modelling using Query likelihood	DNLM
0.01	0.736205539	0.788517548	0.76768341	0.862264349
0.1	0.674231856	0.745941259	0.724450666	0.813317659
0.2	0.654106968	0.673295989	0.683480201	0.736996708
0.3	0.652870386	0.666211395	0.656261048	0.728296238
0.4	0.600086141	0.639949659	0.619683593	0.699085423
0.5	0.587566501	0.62820501	0.615208626	0.686306294
0.6	0.541628181	0.632310059	0.604541939	0.690827911
0.7	0.510531962	0.599050154	0.586735683	0.654412245
0.8	0.473339763	0.570691382	0.559262151	0.62271193
0.9	0.463725261	0.530560081	0.497772722	0.579615886
1	0.263466017	0.451463061	0.419494071	0.373715098

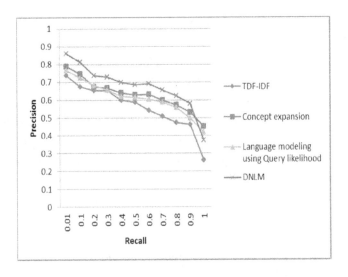

Figure 5.2 Precision values for various techniques for MovieLens dataset

From the Figure 5.2 it is seen that the precision values for DNLM with the proposed concept query expansion is higher than the precision values for tdf.idf by 17% when recall is 0.01 and 25% when recall is 0.9. DNLM with the proposed concept query expansion performs better than concept expansion by 9.3% when recall is 0.01 and by 9.2% when recall is 0.9. Similarly for Language modelling using query likelihood, DNLM with the proposed concept query expansion performs better by 12.3 % when recall is 0.01 and 16.4% when recall is 0.09.

Table 5.2   Average F measure values for various techniques for MovieLens dataset

	TDF-IDF	Concept expansion	Language modelling using Query likelihood	DNLM
F measure	0.528718	0.557951	0.551004	0.575810

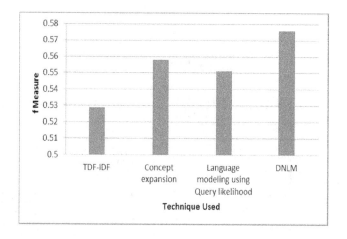

Figure 5.3 Average F measure values for various techniques for MovieLens dataset

From the figure 5.3 it is seen that average f measure values for DNLM with the proposed concept query expansion is higher than the average f measure values for tdf.idf by 8.9%, concept expansion by 3.2% and Language modelling using query likelihood by 4.5 %.

The experimental results for Reuters-21758 dataset for precision and F measure are tabulated in Table 5.3 and Table 5.4 respectively. Figure 5.4 and 5.5 show the same.

Table 5.3 Precision values for various techniques for Reuters-21758 dataset

Recall	TDF-IDF	Concept expansion	Language modelling using Query likelihood	DNLM
0.01	0.831644106	0.89949308	0.875672961	0.983533761
0.1	0.769754052	0.851704269	0.827139846	0.928597104
0.2	0.748400666	0.773306475	0.782014571	0.843243592
0.3	0.748902623	0.764249838	0.755021124	0.835386254
0.4	0.689139901	0.734923375	0.711668277	0.805139854
0.5	0.6774131	0.724206713	0.709199407	0.791218501
0.6	0.627466661	0.732498213	0.700349971	0.801778771
0.7	0.592573475	0.69528761	0.682966143	0.759497059
0.8	0.551441906	0.667393946	0.651598754	0.725531569
0.9	0.543356262	0.620455421	0.582080004	0.677859969
1	0.310100304	0.530449696	0.492848736	0.439102732

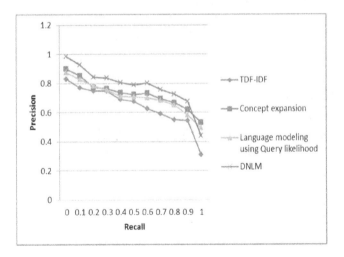

Figure 5.4 Precision values for various techniques for Reuters-21758 dataset

The Figure 5.4 shows the relationship between precision and recall for Reuters-21758 dataset and it is seen that precision values for DNLM with the proposed concept query expansion are higher when compared with the precision values for all the other techniques. The precision values for DNLM with the proposed concept query expansion is higher than the precision values for tdf.idf by 18.2% when recall is 0.01 and 31.5% when recall is 0.9. DNLM with the proposed concept query expansion performs better than concept expansion by 9.3% when recall is 0.01 and 8.7% when recall is 0.9. Similarly for Language modelling using query likelihood, DNLM with the proposed concept query expansion performs better by 12.3 % when recall is 0.01 and 11.3% when recall is 0.09.

Table 5.4   Average F measure values for various techniques for Reuters-21758 dataset

	TDF-IDF	Concept expansion	Language modelling using Query likelihood	DNLM
F measure	0.563152	0.592410	0.585548	0.609676

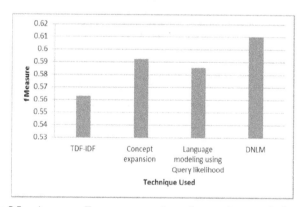

Figure 5.5   Average F measure values for various techniques for Reuters-21758 dataset

135

From the above pictorial representation it is seen that the proposed methodology produces higher average f measure than the existing tf.idf method, concept expansion and Language modelling using Query likelihood. The average f measure values for DNLM with the proposed concept query expansion is higher than the average f measure values for tdf.idf by 8.2%, concept expansion by 2.9%, and Language modelling using query likelihood by 4.1%.

In the second set of experiments, additional terms with query are used. Experiments are conducted for 5, 10, 15, 20, 25 additional terms. Precision values for various techniques for MovieLens dataset and Reuters dataset is evaluated. The techniques used were tdf.idf, Language modelling using query likelihood, proposed concept expansion and proposed DNLM with the proposed feature selection method. The experimental results of percentage improvement for MovieLens dataset and Reuters dataset for precision are tabulated in Table 5.5 and Table 5.6 respectively. Figure 5.7 and 5.8 show the same.

Table 5.5 Percentage Improvement in Precision for MovieLens dataset

Additional terms	Percentage improvement - MovieLens			
	TDF-IDF	Concept expansion	Language modelling using Query likelihood	DNLM
5	2.6	2.32	2.34	2.1
10	3.08	3.07	3.32	3.4
15	3.26	3.42	3.5	3.6
20	3.14	3.02	2.98	2.6
25	2.97	2.7	2.62	2.2

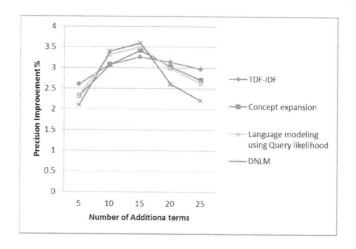

Figure 5.6 Percentage Improvement in Precision for MovieLens dataset

Table 5.6 Percentage Improvement in Precision for Reuters dataset

Additional terms	Percentage improvement - MovieLens			
	TDF-IDF	Concept expansion	Language modelling using Query likelihood	DNLM
5	2.8	2.6	2.74	2.16
10	5.275	5.18	5.12	4.95
15	6.48	6.16	6.39	6.18
20	4.68	4.78	4.32	4.35
25	4.2	4.18	4.57	4.03

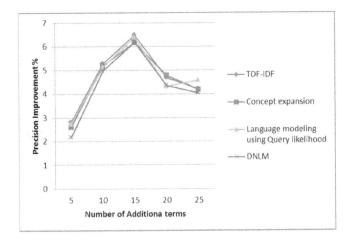

Figure 5.7 Percentage Improvement in Precision for Reuters dataset

5.6 CONCLUSION

In this study, a probabilistic query expansion model is presented based on an automatically constructed similarity thesaurus. A similarity thesaurus reveals domain knowledge about the particular collection from which it is constructed. The two important issues with query expansion are addressed: the selection and the weighting of additional search terms. In contrast to earlier methods, in the proposedmethod queries are extended by addition of terms similar to the concept of the query. Experiments are conducted for varying number of additional terms (5, 10, 15, 20, 25). Experimental results demonstrate the superiority of the proposed concept based query expansion method with respect to the precision. It is also observed that 15 additional terms achieve the maximum precision.

CHAPTER 6

MOBILE AGENTS BASED INFORMATION RETRIEVAL

6.1   INTRODUCTION

As volume of content and content types on internet increases in size it is clear that online publishing needs web content management/ distribution. This study aims to demonstrate information retrieval technology's mobile agent use. It demonstrates workability of this technology combination in e-learning Application.

The Internet is a main source of multimedia content for entertainment, education, and business. Effective or efficient method of data retrieval from Internet is needed and content is an important media in this situation. Humans have amassed enormous amounts of information over time and material is scattered around the world. It is clear that an optimal path to create useful information sources is distribution of the task of digitizing historical and heritage material in analogue formats including books, manuscripts, music scores, maps, photographs, videos, analogue tapes and phonograph records. To achieve this, libraries, museums, and archives globally, large or small, need policies, guidance, and tools to digitize collections to ensure availability economically.

The attraction of this technology for application in distributed digital libraries is its assumption that each system (Content Store) is different. Mobile Agents provide users with "what, where, and how" to access information from systems. Such methods to find out how to access varied archives/collections, each with various database languages and services are both useful and essential as archives/content globally begin to convert collections into digital formats. Despite potential and industry activity, mobile agents were unused in digital library/content domain. Open-source digital library management system 'Fedora' is an exception promoting distributed digital library architecture through operable access to digital objects/ communication across the net based on Web services Agents.

Industry interest resulted in a mobile agents, Web services and related standards development. Though young, adopters are using this technology proving its potential.

6.2   RELATED WORKS

Huang et al (2009) stated a hierarchical mobile agent framework for the high speed and convenience of the Internet in online applications. It was proposed for handling key management and access control problems between mobile agent and host. In advanced networking research, issues on mobile agents have always been of popular interest. Effectively utilizing resources over the Internet greatly enhances the efficiency of an organization and economizes computational overhead. Mobile agents were challenged by execution barriers from security problems. Providing a crypto-system with workable secure-control methods is essential for access activities in the Internet. The procedures of key generation and operation are very simple; users with greater accessibility can directly access the decryption key of the subordinate members, but the latter was not allowed to access encryption key of the former. It economizes the exhaust of storage space. It raises the security of key management, and controls access to distributed environment in non-specific network. It successfully secures the accessing relationship between the mobile agent and the host while economizing the exhaust of storage space.

The achievement facilitates efficient operation of mobile agents, and provides a secure execution environment for mobile computing.

Gao et al (2011) stated an agent migration approach with a multi-agent system to avoid problems like network overload, limited resources of mobile devices, mobile users not always on online during retrieval of data automatically from one or multiple remote biological data sources. To address the above mentioned problems, an agent migration approach with a multi-agent system was integrated to overcome the high latency or limited bandwidth problem by moving their computations to the required resources or services. It also explains the system architecture, the migration strategy, as well as the security authentication of agent migration. The agent migration approach can also be applied to retrieving non-data web resources, for example, sending mobile agents to some bioinformatics web servers and retrieving analysis results to mobile devices. Since user-friendly and publicly accessible web-servers represent the future direction or developing practically more useful models, simulated methods, or predictors.

Fortino and Russo(2012) created an agent called Event-driven Lightweight Distilled State Charts-based Agents (ELDA) Meth, a novel agent-oriented methodology supported by a CASE tool for the simulation-based prototyping of Internet-based distributed agents systems (DAS) that enables rapid prototyping based on visual programming, automatic code generation and dynamic validation, was presented. The distinctive characteristics of ELDA Meth are: effective agent model for distributed computing systems, simulation-based agent-oriented methodology for design validation before implementation and deployment, integration with other methodologies to exploit their well-defined method fragments, and CASE tool support for supporting all development phases from modeling to simulation and implementation. ELDA Meth used both stand-alone for the modeling and evaluation of DAS and coupled with other agent-oriented methodologies for enhancing them with simulation-based validation. In particular, it is based on the ELDA agent model, and provideskey programming abstractions very suitable for highly dynamic distributed computing and on a CASE tool-driven iterative process fully supporting the modeling,simulation, and implementation phases of DAS. ELDA Meth has been applied to prototype several kinds of DAS such as mobile e-Marketplaces, content delivery infrastructures, and information retrieval systems. A case study in the information retrieval domain which has demonstrated the suitability and great effectiveness of ELDA Meth for the rapid prototyping of Internet-based DAS are explained.

Latiri et al (2003) designed an approach for query expansion based on fuzzy association rules between sets of terms. These fuzzy association rules were derived from the corresponding fuzzy closed term sets, which are from the target corpus. Discovered fuzzy contextual inter-term correlations reflect faithfully, the specified terms importance degrees in a user-defined query. To validate this approach, one method was applied to a corpus of the OFIL collection. Information retrieval (IR) focuses on the process of determining and assessing the adequacy between a user-query and a collection of documents, yielding a subset of relevant documents. The query expansion aims to reduce an eventual query/document mismatch by expanding the query using "correlated" terms. An approach based on the use of association rules was proposed to detect such correlations, in order to improve retrieval effectiveness by reducing such mismatch. By considering the term-document relation as a fuzzy binary relation, a fuzzy conceptual approach was proposed to extract fuzzy association rules. An experimental study, on real textual collections, has been conformed intuitive hypothesis that the synergy between association rules and query expansion was fruitful. Results of the study showed a significant improvement in the performances of the information retrieval system, both in terms of recall and precision.

Cui et al (2002) suggested Query expansion as an effective way to resolve the short query and word mismatching problems. The specific characteristics of web searching can be done by web query logs which records the availability of large amount of user interaction information. The gap between the query space and the document space are narrowed. For new queries, high-quality expansion terms can be selected from the document space on the basis of these probabilistic correlations. This method was tested on a data set that is similar to the real web environment. A series of experiments showed that the log-based method can achieve substantial performance improvements, not only over the baseline method without expansion, but also with respect to the local context analysis. New method was proposed to extract probabilistic correlations between query terms and document terms by analyzing query logs. These correlations were then used to select high-quality expansion terms for new queries. The experimental results show that the log-based probabilistic query expansion method can greatly improve the search performance and has several advantages over other existing methods.

6.3   MOBILE AGENTS

Mobile Agents are independent smart programs moving through networks, seeking and interacting with available/compatible services on user's behalf. Mobility is an agent's orthogonal property, as not all agents are mobile. An agent can sit and communicate with surroundings through conventional means like various remote procedures calling and messaging.

6.3.1   Stationary Agents

A stationary agent executes on systems alone, where it begins execution. When information not on a system, is required it needs to interact with agents on other systems. A communication mechanism like RPC is used.

6.3.2   Mobile Agent

A mobile Agent is not tied to a system where it starts execution as it can migrate through a network. Transport ability enables mobile Agents to enter a system having an object with which the agent wants to interact. It takes advantage of being in the source host /network as object.

6.3.3   Characteristics of Mobile Agents

Following are some of the characteristics of Mobile Agents

(i)   Mobile Agents reduce the network load:

In distributed systems, infraction between peer systems relies on communication protocol involving multiple infractions to compete a specific task. Mobile Agents enable packaging a conversation to dispatch it to a destination host, where the infraction takes place locally. When large data volumes scored at a remote server, data should be processed there. Data is located rather than transferred over the Network.

(ii)   Mobile Agents Overcome network latency:

Mobile Agents are dispatched from a central controller to act locally and to directly execute controller directions.

(iii)   Mobile Agents encapsulate protocols.

The code which is incoming/outgoing data encapsulates data itself. When a Mobile Agent migrates it carries data and code interpreting data during communication.

(iv)   Mobile Agents executes asynchronously and atonality

The task to carry out has encapsulations with the agent, which is then dispatched through the network. The connection need not be continuous as it can reconnect at a later time to collect agent.

(v)   Mobile Agent Adapt dynamically:

Mobile Agents can sense their execution environment reacting automatically to changes. Multiple Mobile Agents can distribute themselves among network hosts to maintain optimal configuration.

(vi)   Mobile Agents are Naturally Heterogeneous:

As Mobile Agents transport layer independently being dependent only an execution environment, it ensures optimal conditions for seamless system integration.

(vii)   Mobile Agents are robust and fault Tolerant.

Unfavorable situation/events build robust and fault tolerant distribution system easily.

6.4   MOBILE AGENT APPLICATION

Some of the mobile agent applications are:

(i)   Electronic commerce

(ii)   Personal Assistance

(iii)   Secure Brokering

(iv)   Distribution IR:

IR is an example of a mobile Agent application where instead of moving large data amounts to search engine to create search indexes, it dispatches agents to remote information sources, where it creates search indexes locally to be shipped back to origin later. Mobile Agents perform extended searches not constrained by hours when creator's computer is operational.

(v)   Telecommunication Network Services:

(vi)   Work flow application and groupware

(vii) Monitory and Notification

(viii) Information dissemination

(ix)   Parallel Processing.

6.4.1   Multiple Agents executes a task in parallel: (Remote File Update)

An Agent updates files by replacing one specified word occurrences. The philosophy operating an agent is as follows:

146

It is beneficial for files larger than a specific size (saves network Bandwidth) to perform a distributed files update as it saves file downloading/uploading and distributes update load to multiple servers.

6.4.2 Controlling an Agent

The example discussed has a parent agent that lets its child roam and collect information while on a short leash. Agent's travel itinerary remains with the origin, with parent agent while child agent travels from host to host. The parent agent is stationary, keeping the itinerary of the traveling agent. Itinerary is in destination list. The traveling agent dispatches via proxy for the list's each destination element.

6.4.3 Agent is parallel execution

The Agent delegates tasks to multiple Agents. If an agent searches hosts for information it does either sequentially or parallelly by creating 10 agents (workers) each of whom visits one host.

The parallel execution collaboration scheme is simple. The Agent creates a worker for each destination that he visits. The worker agents are dispatched to respective destinations. Each worker implements task executed by message handler. When it receives a message on completion of task, the worker returns result as a reply to parent agent accommodates incoming results.

6.5 METHODOLOGY

The Mobile agent is a technology needing a "killer application". Though, motions of transportable computer programs or mobile code are around for some time, deployment of technology remains highly limited.

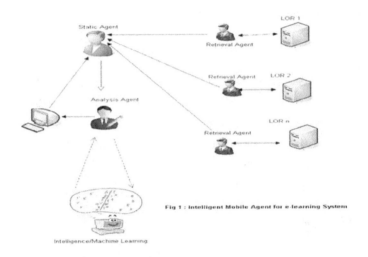

Figure 6.1 Mobile Agents in a Network

Experimental system described here provides concept proof attempting to bring technology deployment closer to reality. Every system has a LMS; a different reformulated query is sent to various systems through mobile agents during retrieval.

Mobile agent's appeal as a distributed computing paradigm, compared to conventional client-server paradigm, is not questioned and is documented. Its deployment not being widespread is due to many reasons, chief of which is that "there is no application that can be implemented only with this paradigm", and so there is no big reason for the paradigm to displace established paradigms like a client-server. One justification to use mobile agent is that paradigm is appropriate to compute on networks with wireless links, as with proper implementation, mobile agents

(i) Allow efficient/economical communication channels use which may have low bandwidth, high latency and be error-prone.

(ii) Enable use of portable, low-cost, personal communications devices to perform complex tasks even when device is not linked to the network.

Another attractive paradigm property is that it allows an application to be really distributed, as tasks in an application, embodied in a mobile agent, are worked out on participating systems in a decentralized process.

Previous chapters reveal that query reformation is effective with use of 15 additional words. Mobile agent concept generates 75 additional words with 5 queries being used by a mobile agent which retrieve query based documents. Retrieved documents median are used as actual retrieved documents.

Experiments are conducted with MovieLens dataset and Reuters dataset and also with college Learning Management System (LMS).

6.5.1 Collection Selections and Ranking

The Mobile Agents play important role in distributed information retrieval for collection selection and ranking problems. The central brokering agent selects only Top N limited number of relevant collections for applying the search according to the given query. The Mobile agents have been already trained with nominal language modelling technique and then they have been migrated to all the document collection in the distributed network and then apply the collection selection and ranking algorithms for the best ranking of relevant documents. The probabilities of a term ti for the given collections Cj have been estimated for each query term using the following formula.

$$P(t_i|C_j) = 0.4 + 0.6 * T * I$$

$$T = \frac{df}{df + + + nw + aw}$$

$$I = \frac{\log \dfrac{|C| + 0.5}{cf}}{\log(|C| + 1.0}$$

(6.1)

where   df   -   number of documents in the Collection C_j

           cf   -   number of collections containing the term t_i

           |C| -   total number of collections

           nw   -   no of words in the Collections

           aw   -   average no. of words of collection being ranked

The result merging is the next step in this distributed information retrieval to combine the result for each query term q and collection C_j to form a belief that a given collection will satisfy the query.

$$W_{jQ} = \sum_{q \in Q} \frac{p(q|C_j)}{|Q|}$$

(6.2)

The results have been analyzed for both the precision and recall for each of the Top N Collections.

6.6   RECOMMENDATION SYSTEMS

Recommendation system is an important e-learning tool, as more institutions implement their features into their learning management system. Recommendation system is planned to overcome the huge data quantities in a dataset. e-commerce is an initial application that used recommender system to increase sales and offers a wide variety of items through the net. e-commerce customers are analogous to learner (student) in e-learning systems. Customer/learner gets recommendations for smart-search.

A recommender system is an information filtering technology designed to determine items most likely to be of the customer (learners) tastes. Recommender system type varies based on affinity between customer and item which is identified with matched pairs. There are two frequently used recommendation system; one being collaborative filtering where a system analyses historical interaction alone, and the other is content based filtering system based on profile attributes.

This study combines hybrid recommendation systems for real world problems. Obtaining recommendation is a critical component in an intelligent decision making system, due to the challenge of personalizing advertising efforts.

It analyses usage data across users to find and match user-item pairs. It collects user feedback as item ratings and exploits similarities in rating behavior amongst many users to determine how to recommend an item.

There are two applications in collaborative filtering

(i) Neighborhood based approaches

(ii) Model based approaches

In neighborhood approach, a user's subset is chosen based on rating similarities. In term such weighted ratings produce predictions for learners.

151

Algorithm 6:

Step1 : Assign a weight to all users based on similarity with active user.

Step2 : Select k top users having highest similarity with active (Neighborhood)

Step 3 : Compute a prediction from a weighted combination of selected neighbors rating.

The $W_{a,u}$ is the similarity weight measure between user 'u' and active user 'a'. The Pearson correlation Co-efficient between ratings of two users is commonly used to find out the weight.

$$W_{a,u} = \frac{\sum_{i \in I}(r_{a,i} - \bar{r}_a)(r_{u,i} - \bar{r}_u)}{\sqrt{\sum_{i \in I}(r_{a,i} - \bar{r}_a)^2 \sum_{i \in I}(r_{u,i} - \bar{r}_u)^2}} \tag{6.3}$$

I – is set of all items

$r_{u,I}$– Rating of user 'u' fir item 'i'

r_u – Average rating of user 'u'.

To produce prediction of recommendation of an item 'i' for user 'a' is generally computed as weighted average of deviations from neighbor's mean.

$$P_{a,i} = \bar{r}_a + \frac{\sum_{u \in k}(r_{u,i} - \bar{r}_u) * W_{a,u}}{W_{u \in k} * W_{a,u}} \tag{6.4}$$

$P_{a,i}$ - Predication for the active user 'a' for item 'i'

$W_{a,u}$ - Similarity between user 'u' with active user 'a'

k – Neighborhood set of most similar users.

6.7 EXPERIMENTAL SETUP AND RESULTS

The Reuters dataset and MovieLens dataset is used for evaluating the proposed methods. The experiments are conducted as detailed in the previous chapter, with the inclusion of proposed concept query expansion method. Precision and recall values for various techniques for MovieLens dataset and Reuters dataset is evaluated. The techniques used were tdf.idf, Language modelling using query likelihood, proposed concept expansion and proposed DNLM with the proposed feature selection method. The experimental results for MovieLens dataset for precision and F measure are tabulated in Table 6.1 and Table 6.2 respectively. Figure 6.2 and 6.3 show the same.

Table 6.1 Precision values for various techniques for MovieLens dataset

Recall	TDF-IDF	Concept expansion	Language modelling using Query likelihood	DNLM
0.01	0.7509	0.8026	0.7838	0.8804
0.1	0.6877	0.7593	0.7396	0.8304
0.2	0.6672	0.6853	0.6978	0.7525
0.3	0.6659	0.6781	0.6700	0.7436
0.4	0.6121	0.6514	0.6327	0.7138
0.5	0.5993	0.6394	0.6281	0.7007
0.6	0.5525	0.6436	0.6172	0.7053
0.7	0.5207	0.6097	0.5990	0.6682
0.8	0.4828	0.5809	0.5710	0.6358
0.9	0.4730	0.5400	0.5082	0.5918
1	0.2687	0.4595	0.4283	0.3816

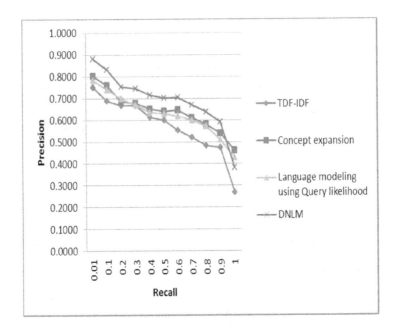

Figure 6.2 Precision values for various techniques for MovieLens dataset

From the Figure 6.2 it is seen that precision values for DNLM is higher than the precision values for all the other techniques. The precision values for DNLM is higher than the precision values for tdf.idf by 17.2% when recall is 0.01and 25.1% when recall is 0.9. DNLM performs better than concept expansion by 9.6% when recall is 0.01and 0.9. Similarly for Language modelling using query likelihood, DNLM performs better by 12.3 % when recall is 0.01 and 16.4% when recall is 0.09.

Table 6.2 Average F measure values for various techniques for MovieLens dataset

	TDF-IDF	Concept expansion	Language modelling using Query likelihood	DNLM
F measure	0.5393	0.5679	0.5626	0.5879

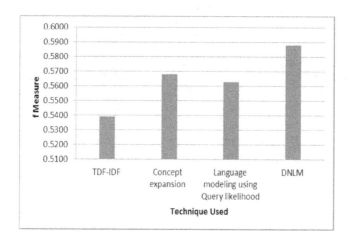

Figure 6.3 Average F measure values for various techniques for MovieLens dataset

From the Figure 6.3 it is seen that average f measure values for DNLM is higher than the average f measure values for all the other techniques. The average f measure values for DNLM is higher than the average f measure values for tdf.idf by 9%, concept expansion by 3.5% and Language modelling using query likelihood by 4.4 %.

The experimental results for Reuters-21758 dataset for precision and F measure are tabulated in Table 6.3 and Table 6.4 respectively. Figure 6.4 and 6.5 show the same.

Table 6.3 Precision values for various techniques for Reuters-21758 dataset

Recall	TDF-IDF	Concept expansion	Language modelling using Query likelihood	DNLM
0.01	0.8491	0.9185	0.8946	0.9909
0.1	0.7859	0.8697	0.8450	0.9355
0.2	0.7641	0.7896	0.7989	0.8495
0.3	0.7647	0.7804	0.7713	0.8416
0.4	0.7036	0.7504	0.7270	0.8111
0.5	0.6917	0.7395	0.7245	0.7971
0.6	0.6407	0.7480	0.7155	0.8078
0.7	0.6050	0.7100	0.6977	0.7652
0.8	0.5630	0.6815	0.6657	0.7309
0.9	0.5548	0.6335	0.5946	0.6829
1	0.3166	0.5416	0.5035	0.4424

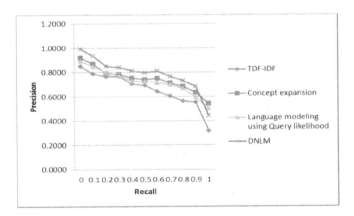

Figure 6.4 Precision values for various techniques for Reuters-21758 dataset

The Figure 6.4 shows the relationship between precision and recall and it is seen that precision values for DNLM is higher than the precision values for tdf.idf by 16.7% when recall is 0.01and 23% when recall is 0.9. DNLM performs better than concept expansion by 7.8% when recall is 0.01and 0.9. Similarly for Language modelling using query likelihood, DNLM performs better by 10.7 % when recall is 0.01 and 14.8% when recall is 0.09.

Table 6.4   Average F measure values for various techniques for Reuters-21758 dataset

	TDF-IDF	Concept expansion	Language modeling using Query likelihood	DNLM
F measure	0.5750	0.6049	0.5982	0.6142

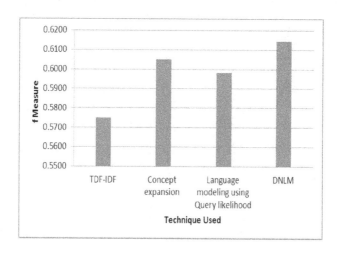

Figure 6.5   Average F measure values for various techniques for Reuters-21758 dataset

The average f measure values for DNLM is higher than the average f measure values for tdf.idf by 6.8%, concept expansion by 1.5 %, and Language modelling using query likelihood by 2.6%.

In the second set of experiments, investigations were conducted in the college Learning management system (LMS) -model which contained html and text based documents (about 15000 pages in 7 subjects).The experimental results for precision and F measure are tabulated in Table 6.5 and Table 6.6 respectively. Figure 6.6 and 6.7 show the same.

Table 6.5 Precision values for various techniques for e-learning dataset

Recall	TDF-IDF	Concept expansion	Language modelling using Query likelihood	DNLM
0.01	0.69361	0.74289	0.72326	0.81237
0.1	0.63522	0.70278	0.68253	0.76626
0.2	0.61626	0.63434	0.64393	0.69435
0.3	0.61509	0.62766	0.61829	0.68615
0.4	0.56536	0.60292	0.58383	0.65863
0.5	0.55357	0.59185	0.57961	0.64659
0.6	0.51029	0.59572	0.56956	0.65085
0.7	0.48099	0.56439	0.55278	0.61654
0.8	0.44595	0.53767	0.52690	0.58668
0.9	0.43689	0.49986	0.46897	0.54608
1	0.24822	0.42534	0.39522	0.35209

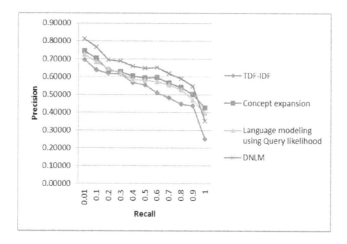

Figure 6.6 Precision values for various techniques for e-learning dataset

From the Figure 6.6 it is seen that precision values for DNLM is higher than the precision values for all the other techniques for e-learning dataset. The precision values for DNLM is higher than the precision values for tdf.idf by 17.1% when recall is 0.01 and 25% when recall is 0.9. DNLM performs better than concept expansion by 9.3% when recall is 0.01 and 9.2% when recall is 0.9. Similarly for Language modelling using query likelihood, DNLM performs better by 12.3 % when recall is 0.01 and 16.4% when recall is 0.09.

Table 6.6   Average F measure values for various techniques for e-learning dataset

	TDF-IDF	Concept expansion	Language modelling using Query likelihood	DNLM
F measure	0.49812	0.52567	0.51912	0.54249

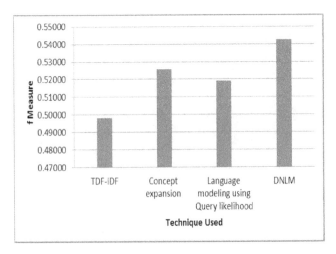

Figure 6.7 Average F measure values for various techniques for e-learning dataset

The average f measure values for DNLM is higher than the average f measure values for tdf.idf by 8.9%, concept expansion by 3.1 %, and Language modelling using query likelihood by 4.5%.

6.7.1 Limitations

The implementation relies on java and itsnetwork support. Hence all participating systems must host a java virtual machine and the extensive java network class library.

System security is a well-known concern for mobile agents. A remote host which allows a mobile agent to visit opens itself to the potential of security breaches. Thus, security levels are required so that the mobile agent is protected from the host, the host is protected from the agent, agents are protected from each other, and hosts are protected from each other.

6.8 CONCLUSION

The objective of this study is to demonstrate the ability of the mobile agent's technology in information retrieval. The system demonstrates the workability of this combination of technologies in an e-learning Application. In the mobile agent concept, 75 additional words are generated and 5 queries are used by each mobile agent. The mobile agents retrieve documents based on the query. The median of the retrieved documents are used as the actual retrieved documents. Experiments are conducted with MovieLens dataset and Reuters dataset. Experiments were also conducted in the college Learning Management System (LMS). Results demonstrate the effectiveness of the mobile agent method.

CHAPTER 7

CONCLUSION AND FUTURE WORK

7.1   CONCLUSION

e-learning has a big role in teaching/learning dealing with multimedia elements like audio, video, animation and images. When information needs to be extracted from a learning object repository (servers), retrieval agents handle activities like sending query to servers/retrieving information. Needed information is forwarded to a static agent, who transforms information to a learner system. If the agent is trained about learning objects retrieval instead of this scenario, it increases precision and accuracy. Instead of retrieving all relevant/irrelevant information from sources, machine learning algorithm is applied to relevant information subset based on concept and mobile agents circulated to information sources to get relevant information alone.

This work suggests a method for Information Retrieval based on Nominal Language Model supporting e-learning environments. A term/phrase has multiple meanings, though a domain specific concept is unambiguous. It is useful to use documents domain specific concepts rather than retrieving documents terms from a specific domain. Thus, concepts list in documents are extracted/annotated with concepts lists. NLM based approach includes natural language processing lexical resources where the process goes through data extraction with a query. Methods of conditional probability theorem determine Affinity rates to ensure this approach is persuasive. Experiments showed that proposed DNLM method achieved better recall compared to traditional tdf.idf and Language modelling using Query likelihood.

A hybrid optimization based feature selection method was proposed to solve nonlinear partitioned clustering problem. The hybrid algorithm is based on PSO and GA. A hybrid approach should have both PSO and GA's merits. PSO's advantage over GA is its algorithmic simplicity and another difference is better convergence control ability. Experiments reveals that proposed feature with proposed DNLM had better recall compared to traditional tdf.idf and Language modelling using Query likelihood.

A similarity thesaurus based probabilistic query expansion model is presented which was constructed automatically. Similarity thesaurus reflects domain knowledge about a specific collection from which it is constructed. Two important issues with query expansion are addressed: selection and weighting of additional search terms. Compared to earlier methods, the proposed method expands queries by adding terms similar to query concept, rather than selecting terms similar to query terms. Experiments conducted for varying number of additional terms (5, 10, 15, 20, 25) and results proved superiority of the proposed concept based query expansion method with respect to precision. It is also seen that 15 additional terms achieve maximum precision.

This study aims to demonstrate mobile agent technology's ability in information retrieval. The system demonstrates workability of this technology combination in an e-learning application. In mobile agent concept, 75 additional words are generated and 5 queries used by each mobile agent. Mobile agents retrieve documents based on query. Retrieved documents median is used as actual retrieved documents. Experiments were conducted with MovieLens dataset and Reuters dataset and also with college Learning

Management System (LMS). Results proved the mobile agent method's effectiveness.

7.2   FUTURE WORK

An elaborate Learning Management System (LMS) dataset needs to be compiled for benchmarking further studies in this research area.

A recommender system incorporating the learner's needs to be further refined.

A benchmark thesaurus would be developed in the lines of WordNet for e-learning research

The research work could be further extended for learning management systems which are deployed in cloud environment.

The algorithms which are proposed in this research work can be incorporated in web service architecture in such a way that the information access or information retrieval will be provided as end learner services to the peer learner community.

The adaptation or the personalization technique can be used in the access or the retrieval of learning content through several soft computing techniques.

The multi linguistic language processing can be used to support multiple languages through which the courses are taught.

APPENDIX – I : Table A.1.1 Literature Survey Research Table I

Sl.No	Paper	Author	Methodology	Objective	Merits	Demerits	My Remarks
01	"Assessment of (computer-supported) collaborative learning, Learning Technologies", IEEE Transactions on, Vol.4, Issue 1, 2011, pp.59-73	**Strijbos, J. W**	Collaborative filtering	Addressing collaborative assessment with a perspective on what is to be addressed	A roadmap is presented as regards the role and application of intelligent tools for assessment	The Content based approaches have not been considered in this work	Both the content based and collaborative based recommendation increases accuracy
02	Analysis of an Agent-based m-Learning System". In Electro technical Conference, 2008, IEEE, pp. 280-285	**Brut, M. M., Sedes, F., and Dumitrescu, S. D.**	Ontology based semantic annotations	With the use of learning objects in Learning management System. Indexing technique for this model's development to acquire better annotations	Uses the Latent Semantic Indexing mathematical approach along with the linguistic-oriented method.	Need to have ontology construction for all the domain	Can go for both linguistic and Word net text processing resource
03	"A logic-based mobile agent programming language for the Semantic Web". Expert Systems with Applications, Vol.38, Issue3, 2011, pp.1723-1737	**Glavinic, V., Rosic, M. and Zelic, M**	Agent based m-Learning System	m-learning as the portable and personal e-learning fashion	Adapt various networks and mobile devices	Propagation delay and consistent network connectivity is needed	We can go for mobile agent system which provides the communication with disconnected architecture.

Table A.1.1(Continued)

04	A common framework for information sharing in e-learning management systems". Expert Systems with Applications, Vol.38. Issue 3, 2011, pp. 2260-2270	**Crasso, M., Mateos, C., Zunino, A., and Campo, M. SWAM**	Prolog based semantic web	Exploits the new web accessible information and services for automated way	Reports examples and experiment results	Dynamism in assessing the document is lacking	Can go for machine learning model for best training
05	Design of a performance-oriented workplace e-learning system using ontology" Expert Systems with Applications, Vol.38, Issue 4, 2011, pp.3372-3382	**Cuéllar, M. P., Delgado, M., and Pegalajar, M. C**	Integration of different heterogeneous LMS	Deals with content dissemination and group works	Discussing the artificial intelligence and knowledge dissemination	Database Schemas allows only structured information access.	Can go and use technique for unstructured information access
06	Ranking Learning Objects through Integration of Different Quality Indicators". Learning Technologies, IEEE Transactions on, Vol.3, Issue 4, 2010, pp.358-363	**Jia, H., Wang, M., Ran, W., Yang, S. J., Liao, J., and Chiu, D. K**	Performance oriented e-learning approach	Increase workplace e-learning practices	The KPI Key Performance indicators have been used to reduce the gap between e-learning organization and individual	This is only the prototype systems	Can go for formal and machine understandable way of conceptualization.

Table A.1.1(Continued)

07	Relevance ranking metrics for learning objects. "Sanz-Rodriguez, J., Dodero, J. M., and Sánchez-Alonso Learning Technologies", IEEE Transactions on, Vol.1 Issue 1, 2008, pp 34-48.	Recommendation of learning objects	Highlights the in sufficiency of current approaches for document clustering	Identify several synthesized quality indicators of learning objects	Not deals with guarantee rating of learning objects	Learning objects should be recommended based on content relevance
08	Relevance-based Retrieval on Hidden-Web Text Databases without Ranking Support Ochoa, X., & Duval, E "Knowledge and Data Engineering", IEEE Transactions on, Vol.23, Issue 10, 2011, pp.1555-1568	Theoritical solution based on relevance ranking	Deals with solution through topical, personal and situational relevance	Consider only the three matrics topical, personal and situational relevance for ranking	Statistical significant ranking have not been considered	Can increase the ranking through combining the metrics with learning algorithms
09	Ranking metrics and search guidance for learning object repository". Learning Technologies, IEEE Transactions on, Vol.3, Issue 3, 2010, pp.250-264 Hristidis, V., Hu, Y., and Ipeirotis, P	IR Style Ranking Function	Query based top ranking	Boolean query source interface	Have not considered the users interest in ranking	Should combine both the content and user based ranking principles

Table A.1.1(Continued)

10	Document clustering in correlation similarity measure space". Knowledge and Data Engineering. IEEE Transactions on, Vol.24, Issue 6, 2012, pp.1002-1013	**Yen, N. Y., Shih, T. K., Chao, L. R., and Jin, Q**	Federated Repository Search ensures the common architecture to discover and share the learning objects	Concept of reusability tree to represent relevant learning objects and its relationships	Considers feedback, weight and degree of relevance	Reweighting of relevance have not been considered.	Ranking can be done by considering reweighs the query term according to its relevance
11	Semi-supervised ranking for document retrieval. Computer Speech & Language, 25(2), 261-281	**Zhang, T., Tang, Y. Y., Fang, B., and Xiang, Y**	Correlation preserving indexing	Correlation similarity measure space between documents were calculated for clustering	Detection of intrinsic geometrical structure of information about the documents helped the ranking	The context based information retrieval have not been considered	Maximize the correlation based on the affinity ratio with respect to the phrase
12	A context-aware adaptive learning system using agents". Expert Systems with Applications, Vol.38, Issue 4, 2011, pp.3280-3286.	**Duh, K., & Kirchhoff, K. (2011)**	Supervised algorithm for classification of text document	Learning to Rank based on the labeled training data with machine learning algorithms	Already deployed on all commercial search engine	Relevance ranking is done based on human annotators only. there is no automated way of annotations	Unlabelled data should also been considered for content classifications.

Table A.1.1(Continued)

No.	Reference	Author	Approach				
13	Structured queries, language modeling, and relevance modeling in cross-language information retrieval". Information processing & management, Vol.41, Issue 3, 2005, pp.457-473	**Yaghmaie M , Bahreininejad**	Multi Agent system using with ontology	Ensures learning content storage, sequencing and adaptations	Implemented on open source platform	Effectiveness and efficiency in access is low	Can use mobile agents rather static agents
14	A mining-based approach on discovering courses pattern for constructing suitable learning path. Expert Systems with Applications, 37(6), 4156-4167	**Larkey, L. S., and Connell, M. E**	Probabilistic Approaches for cross lingual information retrieval	Relevance models exemplified by INQUERY based language model	Unified framework for translation probabilities of cross language information retrieval	Considers only Arabic and Spanish	Can go for any other dataset consist of any documents
15	"Pseudo-relevance feedback and statistical query expansion for web snippet generation". Information Processing Letters, V.9, Issue 1, 2008, pp.18-22.	Hsieh, T. C., & Wang, T. I.	Learning path construction and recommendations	Provides dynamic learning path to the learner based on their own learning styles	Reduces learners time while spending it for searching materials, improves self-directed learning	Mutual relationships between documents were not considered in this approach.	Can use language modeling approach to improve relevance ranking

Table A.1.1(Continued)

16	"An empirical study of query expansion and cluster-based retrieval in language modelling approach". Information processing & management, Vol.43,Issue 2, 2007, pp.302-314.	Ko, Y., An, H., and Seo, J	Statistical query expansion through snippet generation	Ranking of relevant document based on pseudo relevance feedback	Without accessing the document, the document can be marked as relevant/ Irrelevant	The Global dictionary have not used in this approach	Can use word net ontology for query expansions.
17	"Query expansion for document retrieval based on fuzzy rules and user relevance feedback techniques". Expert Systems with Applications, Vol.31, Issue 2, 2006, pp.397-405	Na. S. H., Kang. I. S., Roh, J. E., and Lee, J. H.	Use parsimony query expansion based on clustering algorithms.	Deals with query expansion and dimensionality reduction technique	Unsupervised mode of approach.	Preprocessing of data set	Can use TREC Test Collections
18	"A study of Poisson query generation model for information retrieval". In Proceedings of the 30th annual international ACM SIGIR conference on Research and development in information retrieval 2007 July, pp. 319-326, ACM.	Lin, H. C., Wang. L. H., and Chen, S. M	User Relevance Feedback query expansion method	Calculates the relevant terms of the document's degrees of imports in the document database.	Uses the fuzzy rules to infer the additional query terms and its weights	Fuzzy ness in relevance feedback	Can use hybrid model for query expansion

Table A.1.1(Continued)

19	"Text: Automatic template extraction from heterogeneous web pages. Knowledge and Data Engineering", IEEE Transactions on, Vol.23, Issue 4, 2011, pp.612-626. Mei, Q., Fang, H., and Zhai, C.	Query generation model using Poisson distribution.	The score of the documents have been computed according to the query generation probability model.	Per term smoothing and more accurate background modeling.	Multi stage smoothing is required for higher precision and recall.	Can use multiple criteria for modeling the document.
20	Document language models, query models, and risk minimization for information retrieval. In Proceedings of the 24th annual international ACM SIGIR conference on Research and development in information retrieval (pp. 111-119). ACM. Kim, C., and Shim, K,	Extraction of various templates from the web documents.	Improves the search engine performance, clustering and document classifications	Have used real life dataset for the extraction of templates.	The relationships between the templates are very difficult to be identified.	Can use ontology based on the subject domain.
21	Reducing long queries using query quality predictors. In Proceedings of the 32nd international ACM SIGIR conference on Research and development in information retrieval (pp. 564-571). ACM. Lafferty, J., &Zhai, C. (2001, September).	Basiyan decision theory for document classifications and query modeling	Query language model is evaluated for user preference modeling as regards query, Synonymy and word senses contexts	Markov Chain Link analysis and social network algorithms are used.	Suitable only for short queries.	Can use the world class dictionary suitable to the language of the document for long queries.

Table A.1.1(Continued)

	Reference					
22	A comparative study of methods for estimating query language models with pseudo feedback. In Proceedings of the 18th ACM conference on Information and knowledge management (pp. 1895-1898). ACM. Kumaran, G., &Carvalho, V. R. (2009, July).	Proposed the technique to reduce long queries to effective short ones with out extraneous terms.	Selects top sub query for predicted quality	Converts reduction problem into learning problem	The Average Precision is only 30% in this approach for TREC Data.	Can use the hybrid model which is suitable for both short and long queries.
23	Query likelihood with negative query generation. In Proceedings of the 21st ACM international conference on Information and knowledge management (pp. 1799-1803). ACM. Lv, Y., &Zhai, C. (2009, November).	Estimates query language model with pseudo relevance feedback	Used relevance language model and mixture model for divergence minimization in ranking the documents.	Accuracy is increased due to the mixture model smoothing	Results are heuristics	Can use the statistical distribution technique to improve efficiency
24	Estimation methods for ranking recent information. In Proceedings of the 34th international ACM SIGIR conference on Research and development in Information Retrieval (pp. 495-504). ACM. Lv, Y., &Zhai, C. (2012, October).	They proposed to estimate negative query generation technique	Have used maximum entropy principle for complete query likelihood retrieval.	Reduced Computational costs	The have not considered the positive query generation modeling	Can use mixture model for both positive and negative query generation model

Table A.1.1(Continued)

		Documents	Used the query	Working good	Suitable for	Domain expert
25	Probabilistic relevance models based on document and query generation. Language modeling for information retrieval,13, 1-10. Efron, M., & Golovchiksky, G. (2011, July).	Documents temporal aspects impact the relevancy for certain queries.	Used the query specific information for estimating the parameter for the temporal factor in language modeling	Working good for certain topics with temporal variability.	Suitable for only twitter and newsgroup domain.	Domain expert should be incorporated in to this.
26	PITT at TREC 2012 Session Track: Adaptive Browsing Novelty in a Search Session. In 21st Text REtrieval Conference Notebook Proceedings (TREC 2012). Lafferty, J., &Zhai, C. (2003).	Provided probability semantics unified account underlying language model.	Different factorization of same relevance model.	Involves different component model estimation	Extra evidence in feedback relevant document	Can use model based feedback strategy.
27	A language modelling approach to information retrieval. In Proceedings of the 21st annual international ACM SIGIR conference on Research and development in information retrieval (pp. 275-281). ACM Jiang, J., He, D., & Han, S. (2012).	Adaptive browsing model presented users with relevant and new results in multiple query search.	Combines both browsing model and adhoc search model.	Multi search session	Time delay in ranking	Can do some offline weighting of relevance terms.

Table A.1.1(Continued)

28	Supervised query modelling using wikipedia. In Proceedings of the 33rd international ACM SIGIR conference on Research and development in information retrieval (pp. 875-876). ACM.	Ponte, J. M., & Croft, W. B. (1998, August).	Suggested use of probabilistic language model for investigate text based information retrieval and related issues	Builds language model without the complex semantic model.	Collection statistics used directly in language model estimation	Not considered the concept based ranking	Can go for concept based ranking through clustering
29	"Effective navigation of query results based on concept hierarchies. Knowledge and Data Engineering", IEEE Transactions on, Vol.23, Issue 4, 2011, pp.540-553.	Hsieh, T. C., Chiu, T. K., and Wang, T. I.	Suggested a learning path construction approach based on TF-IDF,ATF-IDF and FCA	Construct the learning concept lattices with keywords of collected documents and then fits the hierarchical relationships among the keywords and concepts	FCA Computes mutual relationships among the documents.	Difficult to construct dynamic learning path	Should use some real online navigation pattern for constructing concept lattices.
30	(An ontological approach for semantic-aware learning objects retrieval. In Advanced Learning Technologies. 2006. Sixths, International Conference on pp. 208-210). IEEE.	Kashyap.A., Hristidis, V., Petropouls, M., and Tavoulari,	Presented a bionav system search interface which enables the user to navigate many query results through MeSH concept	Categorization of bio medical databases and annotations of bio medical citations	Reduce user navigation cost	Very difficult for other domain.	Domain pattern knowledge can be incorporated.

Table A.1.1(Continued)

31	"Assigning Students to Groups Using General and Context-Specific Criteria" Technologies, IEEE Transactions on, Vol.3, Issue 3, 2010, pp.178-189.	Lee, M. C., Tsai, K. H., & Wang, T. I. Learning (2006, July).	Proposed adaptive personalized ranking mechanism to recommend SCORM complaint learning objects from internet repository.	Digital courses have many heterogeneous learning objects	Preference based and neighborhood based approach of ranking	Hard to select Suitable learning objects.		Can combine some machine learning algorithms in ranking the learning objects.
32	"Personalized concept-based clustering of search engine queries". Knowledge and Data Engineering, IEEE Transactions on, Vol.20, Issue 11, 2008, pp.1505-1518.	Hubscher, R.	Method allows instructors to combine a general criterion and context specific preference flexible set to describe group types	Allows students to form their own group based on some general criterion.	Simple and easy to use	Time consuming and sub optimal assignments		Can use some mathematical model

APPENDIX – II : Table A2.1 Literature Survey Research Table I

Title ,Author Affiliation Email	Methods	Objectives	Merits	Demerits	My Remarks
Strijbos 2011	Collaborative filtering	Addressing collaborative assessment with a perspective on what is to be addressed	A roadmap is presented as regards the role and application of intelligent tools for assessment.	The Content based approaches have not been considered in this work.	Both the content based and collaborative based recommendation increases accuracy
Brut 2011	Ontology based semantic annotations	With the use of learning objects in Learning management System. Indexing technique for this model's development to acquire better annotations	Uses the Latent Semantic Indexing mathematical approach along with the linguistic-oriented method.	Need to have ontology construction for all the domain	Can go for both linguistic and Wordnet text processing resource.
Glavinic,2008	Agent based m-Learning System	m-learning as the portable and personal e-learning fashion	Adapt various networks and mobile devices	Propagation delay and consistent network connectivity is needed	We can go for mobile agent system which provides the communication with disconnected architecture.
Crasso,2011	Prolog based semantic web	Exploits the new web accessible information and services for automated way.	Reports examples and experiment results	Dynamism in assessing the document is lacking	Can go for machine learning model for best training

Table A.2.1(Continued)

Cuellar 2011	Integration of different heterogeneous LMS	Deals with content dissemination and group works	Discussing the artificial intelligence and knowledge dissemination	Database Schemas allows only structured information access.	Can go and use technique for unstructured information access
Jia, 2011	Performance oriented e-learning approach	Increase workplace e-learning practices.	The KPI Key Performance indicators have been used to reduce the gap between e-learning organization and individual	This is only the prototype systems.	Can go for formal and machine understandable way of conceptualization.
Sanz-Rodriguez, 2011	Recommendation of learning objects	Highlights the in sufficiency of current approaches for document clustering	Identify several synthesized quality indicators .	Not deals with guarantee rating of learning objects	Learning objects should be recommended based on content relevance.
Ocha, 2008	Theoretical solution based on relevance ranking	Deals with solution through topical, personal and situational relevance	Consider only the three matrices topical, personal and situational relevance for ranking	Statistical significant ranking have not been considered.	Can increase the ranking through combining the metrics with learning algorithms.
Hristidis, 2011	IR Style Ranking Function	Query based top ranking	Boolean query source interface.	Have not considered the users interest in ranking.	Should combine both the content and user based ranking principles.
Yen, 2010	Federated Repository Search ensures the common architecture to discover and share the learning objects.	Concept of reusability tree to represent relevant learning objects and its relationships.	Considers feedback, weight and degree of relevance.	Reweighting of relevance have not considered.	Ranking can be done by considering reweights the query term according to its relevance.

Table A.2.1(Continued)

Zhang,2012	Correlation preserving indexing	Correlation similarity measure space between documents was calculated for clustering.	Detection of intrinsic geometrical structure of information about the documents helped the ranking	The context based information retrieval has not been considered.	Maximize the correlation based on the affinity ratio with respect to the phrase.
Duh	Supervised algorithm for classification of text document	Learning to Rank based on the labeled training data with machine learning algorithms.	Already deployed on all commercial search engine	Relevance ranking is done based on human annotators only. There is no automated way of annotations.	Unlabelled data should also been considered for content classifications.
Yaghmaie,2011	Multi Agent system using with ontology	Ensures learning content storage ,sequencing and adaptations	Implemented on open source platform.	Effectiveness and efficiency in access is low.	Can use mobile agents rather static agents.
Larkey,2005	Probabilistic Approaches for cross lingual information retrieval	Relevance models exemplified by INQUERY based language model.	Unified framework for translation probabilities of cross language information retrieval	Considers only Arabic and Spanish	Can go for any other dataset consist of any documents.
Hsieh,2010	Learning path construction and recommendations.	Provides dynamic learning path to the learner based on their own learning styles	Reduces learners time while spending it for searching materials. Improves self directed learning.	Mutual relationships between documents were not considered in this approach.	Can use language modeling approach to improve relevance ranking.

Table A.2.1(Continued)

KO,2008	Statistical query expansion through snippet generation	Ranking of relevant document based on pseudo relevance feedback	Without accessing the document, the document can be marked as relevant/irrelevant.	The Global dictionary have not used in this approach	Can use wornet ontology for query expansions.
Na,2007	Use parsimony query expansion based on clustering algorithms.	Deals with query expansion and dimensionality reduction technique	Unsupervised mode of approach.	Preprocessing of dataset.	Can use TREC Test Collections
Lin,2006	User Relevance Feedback query expansion method	Calculates the relevant terms of the document's degrees of imports in the document database.	Uses the fuzzy rules to infer the additional query terms and its weights	Fuzzy ness in relevance feedback	Can use hybrid model for query expansion
Mei,2007	Query generation model using Poisson distribution.	The score of the documents have been computed according to the query generation probability model.	Per term smoothing and more accurate background modeling.	Multi stage smoothing is required for higher precision and recall.	Can use multiple criteria for modeling the document.
Kim,2011	Extraction of various templates from the web documents.	Improves the search engine performance, clustering and document classifications	Have used rela life dataset for the extraction of templates.	The relationships between the templates are very difficult to be identified.	Can use ontology based on the subject domain.
Lafferty and Zhai,2001	Basiyan decision theory for document classifications and query modeling	Query Language model is evaluated for user preference modeling as regards query, synonymy, and word senses contexts	Markov Chain Link analysis and social network algorithms are used.	Suitable only for short queries.	Can use the world class dictionary suitable to the language of the document for long queries.

Table A.2.1(Continued)

Kumaran and Carvalho,2009	Proposed the technique to reduce long queries to effective short ones with out extraneous terms.	Selects top sub query for predicted quality	Converts reduction problem into learning problem.	The Average Precision is only 30% in this approach for TREC Data.	Can use the hybrid model which is suitable for both short and long queries.
Lv and Zhai,2009	Estimates query language model with pseudo relevance feedback	Used relevance language model and mixture model for divergence minimization in ranking the documents.	Accuracy is increased due to the mixture model smoothing	Results are heuristics	Can use the statistical distribution technique to improve efficiency
Lv and Zhai,2012	They proposed to estimate negative query generation technique	Have used maximum entropy principle for complete query likelihood retrieval.	Reduced Computational cost	The have not considered the positive query generation modeling	Can use mixture model for both positive and negative query generation model
Golovchinsky,2011	Document temporal s aspects impact the relevancy for certain queries.	Used the query specific information for estimating the parameter for the temporal factor in languag modeling	Working good for certain topics with temporal variability.	Suitable for only twitter and newsgroup domain.	Domain expert should be incorporated in to this.
Lafferty and Zhai 2003	Provided probability semantics unified account underlying language model.	Different factorization of same relevance model.	Involves different component model estimation	Extra evidence in feedback relevant document.	Can use model based feedback strategy.

Table A.2.1(Continued)

Jiang,2012	Adaptive browsing model presented users with relevant and new results in multiple query search.	Combines both browsing model and adhoc search model.	Multi search session	Time delay in ranking	Can do some offline weighting of relevance terms.
Ponte 1998	Suggested use of probabilistic language model for investigate text based information retrieval and related issues	Builds language model without the complex semantic model.	Collection statistics used directly in language model estimation	Not considered the concept based ranking	Can go for concept based ranking through clustering
Meij and De Rijke 2010	Supervised machine learning was used to automatically link queries to Wikipedia articles.	Modeling query concepts via term dependencies ensured great positive effect on retrieval model.	Traditional metrics and diversity measures were noticed.	Knowledge base is required for training the corpus.	Can use some unsupervised algorithms.
Bendersky,2010	Term Dependence model by assigning weights to concepts.	Learning to Rank technique train the model with limited training queries.	Small training samples	External sources of collection have not been considered.	Can combine both endogenous and exogenous features in retrieval effectiveness.
Hsieh,2008	Suggested a learning path construction approach based on TF-IDF,ATF-IDF and FCA	Construct the learning concept lattices with keywords of collected documents and then fits the hierarchical relationships among the keywords and concepts	FCA Computes mutual relationships among the documents.	Difficult to construct dynamic learning path.	Should use some real online navigation pattern for constructing concept lattices.

Table A.2.1(Continued)

Kashyap,2011	Presented a binary system search interface which enables the user to navigate many query results through MeSH concept hierarchy.	Categorization of bio medical databases and annotations of bio medical citations	Reduce user navigation cost	Very difficult for other domain .	Domain pattern knowledge can be incorporated.
Tsai,2006	Proposed adaptive personalized ranking mechanism to recommend SCORM compliant learning objects from internet repository.	Digital courses have many heterogeneous learning objects.	Preference based and neighborhood based approach of ranking	Hard to select Suitable learning objects.	Can combine some machine learning algorithms in ranking the learning objects.
Hubscher,2010	Method allows instructors to combine a general criterion and context specific preference flexible set to describe group types	Allows students to form their own group based on some general criterion.	Simple and easy to use.	Time consuming and sub optimal assignments	Can use some mathematical model.
Leung,2008	Personalized query suggestion based on conceptual preference.	Extracts concepts from web snippets of the search results.	Agglomorative algorithms have been used for clustering related concepts.	Domain knowledge is most important requirement.	Can use some intelligent algorithms for distributed clustering
Iosif,2010	Web based metrics to compute words and terms semantic similarity	Co-occurrence of terms or concepts were analyzed in ranking the results	Without human annotations this method finds the similarity between the documents	74% accuracy in correlation score.	Can use some filtering technique.
Lee,2006	Presented a semantic aware learning object retrieval systems facilitates indexing and searching	Automatic ontology based query expansion.	Ontology should be perfect	Ambiguity in getting the meaning of the query terms.	Can use global dictionary like wordnet.

CPSIA information can be obtained
at www.ICGtesting.com
Printed in the USA
LVHW051128070223
738796LV00015B/1663